SEEING THE FOREST
AND THE TREES

Praise for Seeing the Forest and the Trees

Matthew Lowe demonstrates that life's biggest questions aren't reserved just for philosophers, and I wholeheartedly agree. This book shows how we can think more clearly and creatively about our own lives—and have fun doing it. He reminds us that to err is human, to feel is human, and so too is our capacity to change.

Dr. Yujia Song, Associate Professor of Philosophy, Salisbury University

This book will help to change the narrative of your life! Matthew Lowe is a highly intuitive clinician who uses his years of listening to people to produce a sensible and meaningful pathway for emotional exploration.

Elizabeth Geiling, PhD, LMHC-D, LPC, NCC

Matthew is a skillful guide for anyone wishing to navigate and strengthen the contours of their own mind. Drawing from years of experience with clients, he addresses commonly misunderstood topics such as "overthinking" and "unconditional love." With humor and empathy, Matthew encourages you to follow the threads of your own thoughts to richer and deeper places within.

Dr. Jon Burmeister, Assistant Professor of Philosophy, University of Mount Saint Vincent

This is an engaging, fascinating, and ultimately fun book to read. Matthew offers unique insights, as well as practical guidance in a comfortable and easy-to-read format. This guide is a useful tool for anyone considering participating in therapy, becoming a therapist, or is simply interested in growing and healing as a person.

John McCullagh, PhD, Associate Professor of Psychology, University of Mount Saint Vincent

As a rabbi, I meet people at all stages of life - the highs and the lows, the moments of disappointment, growth, and uncertainty. Matthew Lowe has written a valuable book that gives language and practical support to people as they navigate their personal journeys and seek the support they need in and out of therapy.

Rabbi Suzie Jacobson

This is one of those rare books that can actually change and improve your life—on the inside and out. Truly, a user manual for the way we think and relate to ourselves, Matthew Lowe has created a body of work to return to over and over again.

Howard VanEs, President and Publisher, Let's Write Books, Inc.

Seeing the Forest and the Trees is a masterful guide to navigating the intricate pathways of our inner lives. With profound insights and engaging metaphors, Matthew invites us to zoom in on the details of our struggles while keeping the broader perspective in sight—an essential skill for achieving clarity and fulfillment. As a nature-informed therapist, I deeply resonate with the book's blend of practical wisdom and its grounding in both self-awareness and connection to life's larger themes.

Heidi Schreiber-Pan, Ph.D., LCPC, Author of
Taming the Anxious Mind

SEEING THE FOREST AND THE TREES

Mapping Your Inner World
for Greater Clarity and
Satisfaction in Life

Matthew Lowe, LCPC, MTS

Seeing the Forest and the Trees
Mapping Your Inner World for Greater Clarity and Satisfaction in Life
Matthew Lowe, LCPC, MTS

Published by Matthew Lowe

ISBN: 979-8-218-58917-2

Dedication

To my mother, who has supported and challenged
me on all these topics for decades.

To my father, whose care and humor have influenced
me to take life seriously and light-heartedly.

To Naomi, who is very brave.

Contents

Contents

INTRODUCTION

Seeing the Forest
and the Trees

Mapping Your Inner World for Greater Clarity and Satisfaction in Life

In the middle of the journey of our days
I found that I was in a dark forest,
The right road lost and vanished in the maze.

— The opening line of Dante's Inferno

"There are no wrong roads to anywhere."

— The Phantom Tollbooth, Norton Juster

If you're feeling lost or confused in life, I have two pieces of good news: (1) You're human! (2) You're holding a book full of ideas and recommendations to help you become less often lost and confused and less overwhelmed when you do feel lost and confused.

You can get started right now by asking, "*Where* am I lost right now?" For our purposes, your answer options are: "Lost in the weeds" and "Lost in the clouds." Someone lost in the weeds is so caught up in details that they miss the bigger picture. Someone lost in the clouds is missing those details.

It's a classic both/and situation. Holding both the big picture and the details, taking the views from both above and below is essential. Thus, this book's title, *Seeing the Forest and the Trees*. A balanced perspective can lead to big changes in your life, but it requires the skills of both zooming in and zooming out.

What is it about zooming in and zooming out that's so powerful? To start answering that question, let's enter the dark forest . . .

If I'm not paying attention, it's pretty easy to get lost in the forest. It's one of my favorite places to do two of my favorite things: walking and thinking. I like to stroll along, lost in thought . . . until I look around and realize that I'm lost, literally. Maybe I should be more careful. But, on the other hand, I can also have a good time being lost (though it helps that I tend to hike in areas very close to civilization). Getting oriented is a fun challenge if I have enough snacks, water, and time.

Zooming Out

The fastest and least inventive way to get oriented is to consult a map on my phone (see: hiking very close to civilization). In seconds, I can see myself from above, a dot on a well-labeled map. I can even keep hiking, watching my little dot move, seeing where I'm going and where I might arrive. I know where I am because I know where everything else is in relation to me.

If I'm in a forest with high hills or a mountain, a more strenuous but awe-inspiring way to get oriented is to climb to the highest ground so I can see over the forest. With no obstructions, I can take in the forest as a whole, noticing its topography by watching the crowns of trees roll in waves over the landscape, spotting areas with denser or sparser growth, and maybe spying a road or a town—some marker I can keep in mind as I head back down into the understory.

These views from above can be clarifying but also misleading or dangerous. I'm not proud to admit the number of times I've tripped over roots while looking at the map on my phone, ironically not watching where I was going while I was watching where I was going. I've grossly misjudged distances, wearily discovering that it takes much longer to walk through an area than look over it. It's easy and direct to get somewhere as the crow flies. It's more convoluted as the human treads.

Zooming In

Fortunately, I can also get oriented without the view from *above* the trees by getting oriented *among* the trees. I might remember that moss is more often on the north side of the tree (which receives less sunlight) and that there are usually more branches on the sunnier south side. I can pay attention and notice memorable characteristics of trees—the texture of the bark, the leaves, the colors, whether they rise straight or leaning, have a single trunk or multiple, and if they stand alone or in a cluster. I can start to recognize areas, which is especially helpful in finding out ASAP if I'm walking in circles.

The view from among can also be disorienting, or at least distracting. In a dense enough forest, I can't see very far. I might recognize a spot in the forest, but it's much harder to imagine where I am in the forest as a whole.

Each view, from above or among, has its strengths and weaknesses; together, they are much more powerful. If I can keep my eye on the dot on the map *and* on the trees in front of me, I can look over the trees even while being among them. I can walk more confidently, making my way toward wherever I'd like to be.

Both/And

As a thinker and therapist, I believe people are best served by paying attention to both the forest and the trees in their lives. *Seeing the forest* means trying to look at life and its situations as a whole, to orient oneself to the overarching themes in life—themes like identity, emotion, limitation, goals, relationships, power, and communication. Whatever the situation you're trying to understand, one or more of those themes are always in play, and exploring your relationship to these overarching themes can bring clarity to your specific situation. Once you've mapped out the uphills, downhills, smooth rides, and bumpy rides on your life's path so far, you'll be a little less surprised and a little more prepared when you encounter new ones.

Seeing the trees means paying attention to all the little details and how they interact with each other. For example, if you're having a communication problem with someone, you (and the other person) need to consider how statements, questions, responses, interpretations, emotions, word choices, tones, body language, etc., play interlocking parts in the overall situation. By noticing and tweaking these small details, you can make significant changes to a situation. A realistic solution requires a detailed vision of your situation and its possibilities.

We need to use the forest view and tree view in tandem; by themselves, they are woefully incomplete. Those who see only the forest will bump into trees. Those who see only the trees will have no clue what they're doing in the forest. Someone with both views will feel more capable and less overwhelmed when they encounter problems, whether they're bumping into trees or have utterly lost their way in the forest. By seeing both the forest and the trees, you gain more clarity about yourself, your relationships, and the world around you. With this clarity, you are better prepared to envision what you want, make a plan for pursuing goals and managing obstacles, and thereby gain more satisfaction in your life.

Structure of the Book

This book is a compilation of essays, mostly composed of talking points I've been using with clients over the course of my career as a psychotherapist. I've divided them into six sections reflecting my passions/obsessions in my work: language, limitations, emotions, time and identity, relationships, and how to get the most out of therapy. While I introduce each section through an explicit arboreal metaphor, the essays themselves will demonstrate the forest's and trees' perspectives by playing directly with big ideas and minute details.

So, let's do it! Let's get the lay of the land, *and* let's get into the weeds. Just as Dante found out (and every recovering addict knows), the only way out is through.

How to Get the Most from This Book

You could read it in order, as the sections and chapters are organized intentionally. However, since it is a compilation, feel free to jump around. All chapters (save two) can be read as stand-alone essays. Go to the table of contents and check out whatever piques your interest.

Like with most self-help books, you may get more value from pausing between chapters and doing some self-reflection or talking about it with a friend or therapist. Maybe form a book club just to discuss this book! While any of these options are good for getting the most benefit from this book, I'll admit that I'm the kind of person who just binges on books, so do what you like—I won't judge you.

YOUR WORDS SHAPE YOUR REALITY

"The way we talk about a problem or an issue can determine the solutions we see or don't see. Language shapes our thoughts and our ability to think creatively."

— George Lakoff, American cognitive linguist and philosopher

Abracadabra!

(Traditional magical incantation, sometimes translated as "I will create as I speak.")

It's hard to solve a problem when it has no name. In the muck and mire of sensation, emotion, and inner conflicts, there's no firm place to stand. The right word or idea can make all the difference just by giving you something sturdy by which you can pull yourself up and get unstuck. When you have words for your situation, you can ask questions, seek out insights, and make your way toward solutions.

You're in the forest of language and ideas.

The muddy ground is the stress, the emotional sensations that stick to you and suck you back down when you try to climb out. You need a higher vantage point; you need to climb the trees. The trunks are ideas, and the branches are words.

If you're trying to get somewhere by climbing a tree, there are a lot of factors to consider. Are there branches low enough to grab? Are they strong enough to hold you? Are they too big or slippery to grasp? Do they continue up the entire length of the trunk? If the trunk forks into multiple trunks, which direction do you take?

From the ground, you can't necessarily tell if a tree is climbable. No—the only way to find out is by trying to climb. You can go slowly, testing each branch before putting all your weight on it. Occasionally, you might have to descend a few steps to follow a different set of branches or a different fork in the trunk. You may even need to climb down entirely and start with a different tree.

There is one other major source of help in climbing up a tree—other people. With a friend, you can try out different trunks and branches, then compare notes. Or maybe the friend brought some tools to make the whole thing easier. Or they arrived before you, picked out a strong trunk, and either marked out the best branches to use or installed their own set of rungs. You can follow their way up.

If you're trying to think and talk your way out of a situation, you'll need to take careful interest in ideas and words. Some words are low-hanging branches—a good start, but you may need more words, different words, to get further. Similarly, some ideas are stumps—you can use them, but you won't get far. An idea can take you in the wrong direction entirely—you talk and talk, working your way upward, only to find yourself stuck or in danger (having gone out too far on a limb). Some ideas and words are just too big or too slippery—you want to make sense, but you can't quite grasp it.

You'll need to take an experimental approach, testing out ideas and words, seeing how they feel, seeing where they get you, and being open to going back down and starting over rather than stubbornly clinging to what you've got already. It's helpful to bring a friend to talk it out with. Or ask around and find out who else has addressed the situation. How have others thought and talked their way up and out?

But you'll always need to start by recognizing you're in the forest of language and ideas. Otherwise, you won't deal carefully with your language and ideas. You'll grab whatever's closest, then not understand what went wrong when you come crashing down. You'll need to examine your language and ideas closely—testing them out and trying different ways of speaking the problem—in order to find a viable solution.

The essays in this section are a tour of various regions in the forest of language and ideas. In the first three essays, I survey some of the words that assist with or obstruct our attempts at self-description. In the last two, I lay out thoughts on how to harness ideas about life for personal problem-solving, leading to greater clarity and satisfaction in life.

I'm a Therapist—Here Are the Therapy Words I Have No Use For

Some words sound descriptive and useful but actually do very little to help you understand and change yourself. These words can fail to help by being too vague or ambiguous, by directing you away from a more useful focus of attention, and even by making you feel ashamed. All these problems (vagueness, ambiguity, misdirection, shame) get in the way of productive self-exploration and creative problem-solving.

In this chapter, I share why I find certain words unhelpful and guide you toward more useful language.

Overthinking

The label *overthinking* seems to imply that less or no thinking would be better when what's actually needed is better thinking. *Overthinking* means thinking for a long time (thus the *over* part) but not getting anywhere. The overthinker doesn't get far because their thoughts are repetitive, cyclical, or too narrowly focused. In all cases, these signify that the thinker is having *too few* thoughts and, so, is actually underthinking. They need to think in a way that breaks out of this narrowness.

So call it *underthinking* instead. This identifies the problem in a way that will goad you toward newer, varied, and possibly more useful thoughts.

Acceptance

The word *acceptance* is too ambiguous to be useful. *Acceptance* can mean resignation ("Accept your fate"), affirmation ("Challenge accepted!"[1]), approval/belonging ("You are accepted here"), or acknowledgment ("Accept the facts as they are"). Carl Rogers, one of the founders of humanistic psychology, is known for saying, "When I accept myself as I am, then I can change."[2] But he must be talking about *acknowledging* who he is and not *approving* of himself as is. If he were approving, there'd be no reason for change.

With vague language comes confusion. Stop telling yourself and each other to accept things. Instead, use whatever verb you mean. If you think a certain problem could actually be good for someone, tell them to approve of it. If it's not good for them but definitely needs to be addressed head-on, tell them to acknowledge it.

Confidence/Self-Esteem

Have you ever heard someone say, "If only I were more confident!" They might want confidence to succeed at some public task, such as speaking to a group, socializing at a party, or trying anything new in a place where they might be seen. There are plenty of resources on confidence and self-esteem already, but I find them unhelpful when trying to manage my anxiety. "I'm so anxious" and "I should be more confident" are both statements that keep you focused on yourself. Thus, they can add to the pile-on of paralyzing, self-conscious thoughts. Wondering whether or not you are confident still keeps you stuck in your head and distracted from the actual task at hand.

What do I recommend instead? Don't focus on confidence. Focus on passion! What excites you? What feels so engaging that you lose

1 Bays, C. (Writer) & Fryman, P. (Director). (2011, May 16). "Challenge Accepted" (Season 6, Episode 24) [TV series episode]. In C. Bays (Executive Producer), *How I Met Your Mother*. Bays Thomas Productions.
2 Rogers, C. R. (1995). *On Becoming a Person* (2nd ed.). Houghton Mifflin (Trade).

yourself in it? At a job interview or a public presentation, try to relish the opportunity to talk about something you love, to be asked questions about it—basically, to share your excitement. As far as I know, confident people aren't walking around focused on their own confidence; they're just focused on enjoying and sharing their passions.

Instead of asking, "Do I feel confident with this?" ask, "Do I feel passionate about this?"

Hope

If you are hopeful or want to have hope, I won't discourage it. But as a therapist, I feel ethically obligated not to promise anything about the future. I can't tell you everything is going to be okay because I simply don't know.[3]

I also find that, when someone is overly focused on hope, they end up creating an internal emotional tug-of-war, putting hope in competition with doubt and despair. Because you don't know what will happen next, any insistence on hope can trigger nagging doubts. Now, instead of just feeling hopeful, you're seesawing between hope and despair, often with escalating intensity.

What words would I recommend you use instead? Mostly *desire* and *action*. Desire can persist in the face of despair; you can still *want* even if things seem hopeless. You can still take action, some kind of action, even in the face of despair. Weirdly enough, hope is unnecessary.

I take inspiration for this from Dr. Melissa Raphael's *The Female Face of God in Auschwitz*,[4] in which she documents acts of loving kindness in the concentration camps and people who committed helpful acts of witnessing and being with others, even when no overall salvation seemed possible.

---

3 While I personally do not believe in psychics, I will bring them up as potential resources, given that making promises about the future is appropriate to their field.
4 Raphael, M. (2003). *The Female Face of God in Auschwitz: A Jewish Feminist Theology of the Holocaust*. Routledge.

Deserve

If saying, "I deserve happiness," feels empowering, go for it. But if you're not convinced you deserve happiness, let's focus on a more useful term: *desire.*

Young children, before they've been taught otherwise, simply want. They want what they want because they want it; any question about deserving it arises later in life and only after some other person has taught them to think this way.

To bypass questions of personal value—especially those internalized voices that deny your deserving—return to this original desire. Remember this "for-self-ness" you had (and still have), which wants what it wants because it wants it, regardless of self-critical voices.[5] Don't let *deserve* keep you from knowing your desire.

Willpower/Lazy/Procrastination

What the heck is a will, and where the heck does it get its power? Maybe you've said, "I don't have enough willpower!" Okay, so what's the plan? This word is used so often and yet does very little to clarify how progress is made, slowed, or stopped. Ditto with words like *lazy* and *procrastination.* Both of these words describe a behavioral pattern but do little to clarify the psychological elements in play. They give you nothing to work with to make change.

These terms aren't useful because lack of willpower, etc., isn't an inherent trait. It's a product of conflicts you haven't yet dealt with. When you want conflicting things, it's difficult to act consistently. So, instead, talk about emotional tensions and inner conflicts!

You can make changes only by coming to terms with those conflicts and making an actionable plan for dealing with them when

---

5 I'm not promoting entitlement here. Wanting what you want doesn't actually mean you're entitled to it. My goal here is to help people (usually depressed ones) be more attuned to their desires.

they arise. Relapse is not a failure of the will; it stems from a failure to adequately identify and prepare for complications in the plan. Talk about understanding, preparing for, and committing to your potential discomfort in taking action. Procrastination is almost always motivated by the desire to avoid the uncomfortable emotions that will be stirred up when you take on a difficult task. Identify those uncomfortable emotions and make a plan that involves embracing, tolerating, or at least just working alongside them.

Instead of saying, "I'm lazy, etc.," say, "I'm conflicted."

I won't . . .

"I didn't do anything this past weekend" is not descriptive. It's the opposite of a description. How would you draw a picture of someone not doing anything? Even "I just sat around" is more descriptive. Similarly, "I won't smoke" sounds like a plan, but it's the opposite of a plan. Can you draw a picture of someone not smoking? If you can't actually imagine an alternative, you don't have one.

So, what words do I recommend instead? Say what you actually did. Say what you'll actually do. Make a plan with actionable steps. "When I feel like smoking, I will do x,y, and/or z instead." Only then do you have a plan to work with.

Other Problematic Words and Phrases Addressed Elsewhere in This Book

- Selfish/Selfless: (See "Should you be selfish or selfless? Neither—It's time to self-inhabit" on page 133.)
- Gaslighting: (See "From Gaslighting to Intersubjectivity: How to Stop Driving Each Other Crazy" on page 156.)
- "I wish I didn't care so much": (See "Do You Care Too Much? Embrace Tiredness!" on page 90.)
- "They did that for no reason": (See "Everything People Do Makes Sense (Even the Nonsense)" on page 137.)

Conclusion

Words matter! They are the handholds and signs you use as you try to feel your way through life, and the vague or inaccurate ones will lead you in the wrong directions. If your thought process isn't getting you anywhere, it may be time to examine the words you're using and try out some new ones.

You Can't Think Clearly with Confusing Language

Introduction

It's one thing to have an experience and another thing to have a word for that experience. I remember having a friend—well, sort of a friend. They were friends with my friends, and sometimes we were friendly, but other times, it felt like they were out to get me. I just didn't understand this relationship . . . until I was given the word *frenemy*. *Aha! That's what they are!* I thought. To have such a specific, granular word whose meaning captured my feeling was liberating and empowering.

The power here wasn't just in the word *frenemy* but in the clarity that came when placing it next to all the other words I already had for social relationships—*friend, enemy, stranger, acquaintance, casual friend, foil*, etc. Knowing what a frenemy is requires knowing what it isn't—knowing the difference is what allowed me to start figuring out exactly what to do with a frenemy.

You need more words. But specifically, you need to know the differences between words. Without more words, ideas and experiences get lumped together, which keeps you confused. The more you can get specific, the more you can understand yourself and express what you need.

In my work as a cognitive therapist, I'm very focused on language, and many of my interventions with clients consist of introducing new vocabulary and new distinctions. Here are some of the words and distinctions I find myself sharing often:

19

Self-Image

Humiliating	Humbling
"OMG, I'm the worst."	"Oof! I have limits to work on and/or allow."

This distinction matters because . . .

These are very different ways of feeling bad for/about yourself. Humiliation is a debilitating emotion not unlike shame. The humiliated person gives up on themselves and then avoids the challenging situation. On the other hand, being humbled is a step toward developing a realistic and compassionate sense of self, toward acknowledging and working with temporary or permanent limitations. The humbled person does not give up on themselves.

Stop Sign	Hurdle
"I can't/shouldn't keep doing this!"	"Getting through this will make me stronger!"

This distinction matters because . . .

Okay, these aren't words usually put together, but they capture a distinction worth highlighting: When you're pursuing a goal or relationship and encounter a very difficult challenge, should you see it as a sign to stop or a hurdle to overcome?

Mistaking a hurdle for a stop sign is how you can end up quitting relationships prematurely. Maybe you could learn to compromise about which movie to see instead of just breaking up over it. Mistaking a stop sign for a hurdle is how you injure yourself by violating your own boundaries. Perhaps you should have called it quits after they cheated again instead of insisting to yourself that love conquers all.

Both stop signs and hurdles exist, and you need the wisdom to tell the difference between the two. So, how do you tell the difference here? I don't know if you can ever be sure, but it seems best to pay attention to your experiences of progress, pain, and danger. When you're pushing yourself past boundaries, ask yourself, (1) "Is this pushing getting me anywhere?" and (2) "Does it feel safe to keep pushing?"

Describing Independence in Relationships

Secrecy	Privacy
"I don't want them to know because I'd be in trouble if they did."	"I don't want them to know because it's mine, and I don't need them to know it."

This distinction matters because . . .

Negotiating trust and independence is an essential task in any partner relationship. Secrets hide a betrayal of trust; private matters do not. Unfortunately, these two terms often get lumped together, especially when jealousy (see below) is involved, with one or both partners seeing the other's independence as a threat to the relationship. Consider which of these statements sounds healthy and which is a red flag: (1) "We have no secrets in this relationship." (2) "I have no privacy in this relationship."

Envy	Jealousy
"You have it, and I want it."	"I have it, but it could be taken away."

This distinction matters because . . .

Both envy and jealousy describe emotional states in which you value something but feel insecure about it. In envy, you value something but don't have it; in jealousy, you value something but worry about whether you'll be able to keep it. It's helpful to recognize the difference so you can be more sensitive to yourself when trying to address your insecurities. If you realize that you're captivated by envy, you can focus more on what you already have and what you can realistically pursue. If you realize that you're captivated by jealousy, you can focus on the relationship you're worried about and find ways to strengthen it rather than frantically acting out your fear of loss.

Relational Communication

Validate	Empathize
"You're right to feel this way. I'd feel that way too."	"I understand why you feel this way."

This distinction matters because . . .

Sometimes, others want your support but you don't feel comfortable giving it wholeheartedly. When you don't want to validate how someone feels, it's too easy to revert to attacking the other's feelings—a move that serves neither the person nor the relationship. Good news: You can empathize with someone without explicitly validating their opinion! "That must've been [insert emotion here]" helps the other person feel felt without requiring you to betray your own perspective.

I'm sorry (Moral guilt)	I'm sorry (Sympathetic "guilt")
"I feel bad that I caused the problem."	"I feel sad about your situation."

This distinction matters because . . .

I'm not suggesting that we do away with the phrase *I'm sorry*, but recognizing the difference can alleviate unwarranted guilty feelings. This is especially important when you are conflicted about doing the right thing if it could make someone else feel bad. I'm specifically thinking about the challenge of setting boundaries in relationships. "I feel sad that they will feel bad" is different from "I shouldn't make them feel bad." Confusing sympathy with guilt is how you end up violating your own needs to protect another's feelings.

Conclusion

There are many more distinctions like this explored in this book:

- The difference between selfless, selfish, and self-inhabiting (see "Should You Be Selfish or Selfless? Neither—It's Time to Self-Inhabit" on page 133).

- The difference between doubt and despair (see "Despair is Part of the Process" on page 87).
- The difference between a good cry and a bad cry (see "How to Have a Good Cry (And Avoid a Bad Cry)" on page 96).

The more words you have, the more distinctions you can make and the more specific you can be in understanding and planning your life.

Words People Use When They're Almost (But Not Quite) Ready to Think Deeply About Themselves

While they might know *something* is wrong, many people show up to therapy with vague senses—a vague sense of what's going on inside themselves and a vague sense of what they want. And because they feel so vague, they use vague language.[6]

Vague language is . . . well, it's a good place to start. Imagine you're a guest in my house and ask where the bathroom is. The most precise directions would lead you directly to the doorknob. Vague directions might get you to one of the walls outside the bathroom. If you've found a wall, you still haven't found the door, but you're getting closer. (Although, in the case of the bathroom, let's recognize that close isn't quite good enough!)

Now imagine it's the middle of the night and you're feeling around in the dark, trying to find the bathroom. Find a wall, and you'll keep feeling around for a door. But maybe you're on the wrong wall. Or you find the door, but you can't understand how it opens (like when doors slide instead of being pushed in or out)! At a certain point, you might just give up altogether. Vague language has unfortunate consequences!

In my time as a therapist, I've started recognizing certain vague words and phrases clients use when they want to explore themselves

6 Bandler, R. and Grinder, J. (1975). *The Structure of Magic I: A Book About Language and Therapy.* Science and Behavior Books.

and their options but can't quite find their way in. These words and phrases can function as an outside wall to a room—that is, they tell you you're getting close even while continuing to keep you out.

I'm hoping this list will help you recognize when you use them and provide guidance in helping you move from the wall to the door. You can turn these wall words into doorways, which allow you to step through and see what's on the other side.

"That was interesting"

To call something interesting is not being descriptive. Literally, you're only saying that it catches your interest. It's not unlike remarking that something is remarkable. Okay, you've remarked on it, but you haven't really said anything! And yet, there must be something more to your experience here, given that it's caught your interest.

If you find yourself calling something *interesting*, a few follow-up questions will help you turn this wall into a door:

- "Interesting good or interesting bad?"
- "What's interesting to me about it?"
- "Okay, so it's interesting—is there another adjective that could more accurately capture my observations and experience?"

"That was weird"

To call something weird is very similar to calling it interesting, except with a twist: You're more likely to use *weird* (instead of *interesting*) when you're having a new or bad experience. You call something weird when it makes you feel weird. The word implies some kind of unclear or uncomfortable feeling. A new experience, even a good one, is still weird simply because it's outside your normal. You may call a bad experience weird when you can't yet name what you don't like about it.

Sometimes, you use *weird* when you *do* know how you feel but don't *want* to give it a more specific word. If you say you had a weird time at the party, you might be avoiding naming that you felt alienated, annoyed, embarrassed, and other specific feelings that, once named, might become more intense. It can feel safer to use *weird* than to label (and possibly amplify) negative feelings.

But . . . if you want to explore your experiences, you'll need to lean into the discomfort, turning the door into a wall. You can elaborate on *weird* by using the same questions as above, replacing *interesting* with *weird*.[7]

"I don't know how to feel about this"

This phrase functions as a *wall* because you know a feeling should be part of your experience, but your emotional awareness is vague or confused. Why would someone feel vague or confused about their emotions?

A few overlapping possibilities:

1. You don't have a word to capture your feeling; the fancy therapist term for this is *alexithymia*.[8] In alexithymia, you may experience emotions purely in your body, or you might just say you feel off. You might not know how to go about finding words to express your feelings. You've hit a wall in your vocabulary.

2. You assume your emotional state must be captured by *only one* emotion word. I'm not sure where this assumption comes from, but maybe it's because the question "How do you feel?" seems to call for a single or simple answer instead of a multiple or complex one. You hit a wall when you don't yet see that it's appropriate and okay to have multiple feelings in response to something.

---

7 A friend has pointed out that *crazy* can serve as a similar filler word, which can be used to label experiences ranging from chaotic and uneasy to fun, weird, and interesting.

8 Created by psychiatrists John Case Nemiah and Peter Sifneos from Ancient Greek ἀ- (a-, "not") + λέξις (léxis, "speaking") + θυμός (thumós, "heart"), meaning "without words for emotions." "Stichwort Alexi | thymie". Duden. Das Wörterbuch medizinischer Fachausdrücke. Software für PC-Bibliothek. Mannheim: Bibliographisches Institut.

3. You assume there's a *right* way to feel, but you're not feeling it. This usually comes up on occasions that are "supposed" to be happy or sad. When someone says, "I don't know how to feel," the sentiment may actually be "I know I'm supposed to be happy, but actually, I'm scared," or "I know I'm supposed to feel sad, but actually, I'm relieved." When you don't feel what you're "supposed" to feel, you might feel guilty—and it's more comfortable to feel confused than guilty.

You can use this phrase as a door by recognizing that "I don't know how to feel" usually indicates more than one feeling or a feeling you're hesitant to acknowledge or validate. Maybe it would be easier to try to name a few emotions instead of needing to settle on one. Or, if you feel conflicted about your emotions, say you feel conflicted.

Which brings us to . . .

"Stuck"

This word shows up when you're trying to figure out what to do in a situation, and you feel either stuck with a single option or stuck between multiple options. You want to move forward but feel like you can't.

If you feel stuck and don't know why, try the following questions to expand the metaphor. (For more on expanding metaphors, see page 42.)

- "Stuck between what?"
- "What's so sticky about my situation?"
- "Why am I stuck to this? Why is this stuck to me?"

Or maybe you feel stuck and know exactly why you feel that way. Stuckness can capture the experience of "I want conflicting things" or "I want something, but I'm afraid to want it." Either way, in order to get unstuck, there are two tasks at hand—one rational and the other emotional:

- *Rational*: Make pro/con lists for each option. Now you can look at them from above, consider each as a package deal, and consider which cons you are willing and able to tolerate. Even if this doesn't help you make the decision, jotting the conflict down on paper can help it feel less intense than just holding it in your head.

- *Emotional*: Honor your stuckness as a sign that you are a limited and complex human being. (For more, see "You Are a Limited Person (And So Am I)" on page 65.) With limited knowledge of the future and conflicted feelings about your options, it makes sense to feel stuck! It's okay to hate the feeling as long as you don't hate yourself for feeling stuck. Getting unstuck will require acts of courage to head out into the unknown or sacrifice some part of yourself in the process of making the decision.

Exasperating Rhetorical Questions

Rhetorical questions function as a *wall* because they are opinions masquerading as questions. "What the heck is wrong with that guy?" usually means "What they're doing is wrong and unjustifiable!" "What were they thinking?" usually means "What they did makes no sense!" Rhetorical questions indicate a current dead end in thought and communication. Despite asking a question, you're not really curious.

Rhetorical questions can function as a *door* when you take them literally:

- "Wait, I should sincerely ask that question. What, indeed, were they thinking?"
- "No, really. What is my problem?"

Try to answer those rhetorical questions. You'll get further.

Conclusion

If you're trying to talk your way through something, you have to start somewhere. These kinds of vague phrases often come to mind first. They're not a bad starting point, but only if you notice that you're using them, recognize them for what they are, then take steps to move beyond them.

To Understand Your Life, Think BIG

Big Questions, Big Words

Your questions about life are always more interesting than any answers you find. How can I tell? Because asking questions opens you up to exploration and conversation; an answer often shuts them down. Because one question can lead to many answers. Because when you return your attention to any big topic about life (see below), you're returning to the questions, not the answers. Even an interesting answer—some truly fascinating conclusion about life—can only arise from a good question.

When you're asking questions about life, what specifically are you asking about? I'd say you're asking about your relationship to one or several Big Words. What do I mean by a Big Word? Something so important that we thinkers feel compelled to write it down with capital letters. I'll list some of the Big Questions, then some of the Big Words that lie underneath those questions.

- Big Question: "What is the meaning of life?"
  Big Words: *Meaning, Purpose, Value, Spirituality*

- Big Question: "What will I do with my life?"
  Big Words: *Time, Freedom, Choice, Identity, Purpose, Legacy, Personal Narrative*

- Big Question: "Will I be okay?"
  Big Words: *Future, Health, Strength, Vulnerability, Emotion, Loss, Hope, Lifestyle, Fate, Social Position, Environment*

- Big Question: "Am I a good person? What's the right thing to do?"
  Big Words: *Right, Wrong, Ethics, Morals, Obligation, Justice, Courage, Action*

- Big Question: "What will I do with the people around me?"
  Big Words: Relationships, Communication, Community, Citizenship, Belonging, Love, Connection, Disconnection, Cooperation, Competition

Regarding each of the Big Words above, further questions always apply along the lines of "What is ___ to me?" and "What will I do with my concerns about ___?"

Most Big Questions Start Out Small

Of course, you don't live life in the abstract. So, it's rare that "What is the meaning of life?" is the first and central question on your mind. Here's what actually happens: A concrete question arises in a particular situation, and some Big Questions lurk underneath it. When folks wonder if they should apply for that job, if they should stay in or go out tonight, or why that pet food commercial made them cry, they are all asking questions that, if explored deeply enough, will lead to questions about meaning in life.

Similarly, you'll find that mundane situations can all be viewed as being about Big Words. It's a common TV trope known as "It's the Principle of the Thing."[9] That's when a character makes a big deal of a

---

9 *It's the Principles of the Thing.* TV Tropes. Retrieved August 31, 2024, from https://tvtropes.org/pmwiki/pmwiki.php/Main/ItsThePrincipleOfTheThing

seemingly trivial situation because, to them, the stakes are deeper than others realize.

Here's a mundane example I'll build on later: You're at a restaurant, and the service has been terrible. You're dissatisfied and annoyed, and you want to do something about it. Here are some of the little questions in play:

- What was wrong with the service?
- Why did it bother you this much?
- What would you like to do about it?
- What are your options, and how do you feel about them?

Based on how you answer, some or all of the following Big Words may be in play here:

- *Fairness*
- *Justice*
- *Rights*
- *Self-Respect*
- *Communication*
- *Social Norms*
- *Action*
- *Consequences*

Your beliefs about these Big Words play a role in your assessment and decision-making in the situation, whether you're aware of them or not. If you can examine these Big Words and your beliefs, you'll be better able to think and plan your way through the situation. A foray into the abstract can clarify and inform your thoughts about the mundane. Someone insisting, "It's the principle of the thing!" would do well to examine those principles.

Everyone's a Philosopher

All these Big Words are indeed massive topics, and that's the point. Each one can be overwhelming to think about—even more so when you realize that these words are often interconnected. It's hard to explore one without bumping into several others.

But to address one of the main reasons this is so overwhelming, let's name the word I've been avoiding so far: *philosophy*. I've been avoiding it because the word is such a turn-off for people. It conjures up navel-gazing, ivory-tower intellectuals talking endlessly, getting nowhere, and losing touch with how most people think about life.

But I should be clear that this whole essay is a plug for philosophy . . . just not the academic kind.

So, what's philosophy? Here's my short version:

- *Philo* (Greek) = Love
- *Sophia* (Greek) = Wisdom
- Wisdom = Thoughts and beliefs about how best to do anything, including live life

So, if you're trying to figure out how best to live your life . . . you're a philosopher whether you like it or not. Sorry?

Now then, if you're a philosopher, no matter what, and philosophy is overwhelming, what now? I want to offer some initial ideas on how to think about big questions without getting overwhelmed.

"Doing" Philosophy Without Reading Philosophy

First, give up hope of finding absolutely perfect answers.

Why?

- These questions are bigger than you, and they've been around a super long time.

- They will keep coming up again and again in your life, given that where you are in life is going to impact how you feel about the questions and how you answer them.
- Whatever answers you settle on, they're very likely to be the ones that work for you rather than absolute answers that work for everybody.

Second, recognize the answers you've already been living.

What?

- One very authentic answer to a Big Question is "I don't know!" Not having a clue is a valid stance toward Big Questions about life. (For more, see "How to Be Good at Being Clueless" on page 67.)
- Lived answers are the ones implied by your thoughts, feelings, and actions so far in life. Let's say you're trying to answer the question "What will I do with my life?" Start by asking, "What have I been doing with my life so far?" Similarly, you should ask, "*Where* do I already find meaning in my life? *When* have I felt like a good person?" And so on.
- Once you recognize your lived answers, you can reflect on how you feel about your lived answers. Are they working for you?

Third, brainstorm new answers and see what you find attractive or realistic.

How?

Some introductory strategies: Write it out, talk it out, or take a break.

- Write it all down: Write out the question and all you've thought about it already. I recommend doing this in bullet-point form. It doesn't need to flow or be organized. Do this until you hit a wall—until you're not sure where and how to proceed. Now ask yourself one more question: "What makes this so hard to figure out?"

- Talk to more people about it: One of my favorite ways to think outside the box is to recruit someone else who's already outside the box, a.k.a. outside my head. Between the two (or more) of us, new answers can arise.
- Think about it for a while, then take a break: Insights sometimes happen when we're not overly focused. See shower thoughts (a sudden idea that occurs during an unconnected, mundane activity)[10] and other distractions[11] that can provoke insights.

Some More Advanced Strategies: Analyze, Fictionalize, Stumble Forward

These strategies focus on how to pick apart and play with possibilities, and each can build off the other. I'll share what each generally means, then use the bad restaurant scenario to demonstrate.

- Analyze: Look at the mundane situation and identify the Big Words (a.k.a. important concepts) involved.
- Fictionalize: Ask, "What would someone else think and do in this situation?"
- Stumble forward: Generate half-baked solutions and tweak them.

Analyze

In the bad restaurant example, I identified some of these Big Words that could be involved: Justice, Self-Respect, Respect, Communication, Social Norms, etc. When you have these words in mind, you can consider how they may be interacting and conflicting. Yelling at a waiter may help you assert Self-Respect, but does it show Respect to

---

10 Collins Dictionary, s.v., "shower thoughts," accessed March 17, 2024, https://idioms. thefreedictionary.com/own+it
11 Marshall, C. (2015, February 11). Why you do your most creative thinking in the shower, car, or bed. Boing Boing. https://boingboing.net/2015/02/11/why-you-do-your-most-creative.html

the waiter? Quietly complaining or leaving a bad Yelp review may be a form of Communication, but will you feel like Justice has been served? By sorting through these Big Words, it becomes clear that you prefer options that honor as many of your values as possible.

Fictionalize

Take the fictional approach by telling yourself a story about how other characters would deal with the situation. Think about situations involving Justice, Self-Respect, Communication, etc. What would Jesus do? What would Miss Piggy do? What would [some other personal, public, real, fictional role model] do? Each person's perspective and action reflect a different philosophy of the situation, and taking those into consideration can help you recognize where your own philosophy stands. By thinking of a variety of fictional possibilities, you can develop a greater awareness of all the variables involved—that you might complain or not, that you might speak calmly or angrily, that you might be angry at yourself, the waiter, the cook, the owner, or the world in general.

Stumble Forward

Now that you've done some analyzing and fictionalizing, you have some ideas to work with as you stumble forward into new interpretations and solutions. What about Jesus's approach would work for you, and what wouldn't? Ditto with Miss Piggy and so on. What if Jesus and Miss Piggy collaborated on this problem? How might they compromise on a solution? For any answer, assess its strengths and weaknesses, then come up with new answers that address those weaknesses. Do the same with these new answers.[12] The more answers you generate, the better the chance you'll arrive at something you like. You can stumble forward into something that works for you.

---

12 For the philosophical deep end of this approach, google "Hegelian dialectic."

Conclusion

Admittedly, this all serves as a shallow and brief introduction to a deep and lengthy topic. Philosophy (and philosophers) tend to go on and on and on, an endlessness that is both appropriate to the subject and not very useful to the nonacademic philosopher. If you're fishing for wisdom in a vast ocean of thoughts, it's easier to start by learning to sail around, survey the territory, and skim the surface. You're less likely to drown this way.

But you do have to go deep, at least somewhat. Fish (insights) rarely leap into the boat. Perhaps, in your search for wisdom, you'll need an approach that allows you to alternate between the deep and the shallow end. Analyzing concrete situations (shallow end) can point you toward abstract topics (deep end), but these abstract explorations are useful only if they help you deal with the concrete, a.k.a. actual life.

I'm hoping that the tools I've surveyed here allow you to do just that—explore the questions in your life by exploring the questions of life without getting lost. Let's move this fishing/ocean metaphor back onto dry land, where you can explore specific situations (trees) by looking at the bigger picture (the forest).

So, try some of it out! The steps above are a place to start. (And honestly, a place to end if the thought of further exploration sounds exhausting and/or annoying. For more on embracing tiredness, see "Do You Care Too Much? Embrace Tiredness!" on page 90.) Either way, amateur philosophizing can help you appreciate the big questions about life and feel like you can think about them without *too* much stress.

To Understand
Your Life, Think About
Something Else!

Telling It Slant[13]

Sometimes, life can be overwhelming to think about head-on. From a fixed perspective, your problems keep looking the same, your ability to generate solutions remains limited, and misery feels unavoidable. You want to make progress, but it's hard to lay new rails for your train of thought, so there you go, driving yourself into walls, around in circles, and off cliffs. It can be emotionally intense to think about life, so you might overheat and break down as well.

Maybe another approach is needed—something creative enough to get you somewhere new in your thinking and something playful enough to take some of the emotional edge off self-reflection. You need metaphors.

Metaphors! They're clever, fun, weird . . . and very useful for personal problem-solving. When your train of thought is overheating and crashing, a metaphor is a great tool for jumping track and taking wild detours to reach insights and decisions inaccessible by straightforward approaches.

---

13 Dickinson, E. (1999). *The Poems of Emily Dickinson: Reading Edition*. (R.W. Franklin, Ed.). Harvard University Press.

How Metaphors Work

First, a basic definition: Metaphor is understanding one kind of thing in terms of another.[14,15] Here are five you're probably familiar with:

- Love is a battlefield.[16]
- Cut me some slack!
- I feel like a couch potato.
- I can't wrap my head around it.
- You hit the nail on the head.

In each one of these, something abstract—love, discipline, sense of self, understanding, or making a point—is compared to something more concrete—battles, boating, potatoes, wrapping, and hammering. Once the two things are connected in your mind, you're able to explore the abstract topic by playing with the concrete one.

Let's use "Love is a battlefield" to see how this works. When you think about battles, what comes to mind? I think of allies, enemies, soldiers, ammunition, targets, going nuclear, conquering, civil war, making peace, etc. Now then, if love is a battlefield, what are the sides? Who are the soldiers, what is the ammunition, etc.? What causes war between nations, and is it similar to what causes war in your relationships? How do nations move from war to peace? Can any of those moves be translated into advice about making peace in your relationships?

Neat, right? It's all very clever to use imagination to understand and solve problems. It's clever, but maybe you're wondering, *Shouldn't self-reflection be a little more emotional than this?*

---

14 Lakoff, G., & Johnson, M. (1981). *Metaphors We Live By*. University of Chicago Press.
15 Let's get this out of the way now—a simile is not different from a metaphor. It's just a kind of metaphor (specifically the kind that uses *like*). Other types of speech that use a metaphorical style: analogy, allegory, parable, fable.
16 Pat Benatar. (1983). "Love is a Battlefield" [Song]. On *Live from Earth*. Chrysalis.

And that's the genius here. The right metaphor creates a unique therapeutic (growing/healing) experience in what I'll call the Goldilocks zone[17] of emotional vulnerability.

Why Metaphors Work

A metaphor is an intellectual exercise, which makes it stimulating and distracting, giving you distance from the emotional intensity of the actual situation. It's hard to analyze anything when you're overwhelmed, and the introduction of play interrupts that feeling of overwhelm. Because it's *interesting* to compare love to a battlefield, the effort to expand the metaphor engages your *curiosity* and *inventiveness*. Curiosity is itself an emotional state, but a very different one from the yearning/heartache evoked by the actual situation. By lowering your emotional intensity, you are freer to explore.

So, yes, using metaphor makes your experience less emotional, which makes it easier for you to analyze and get insight into an emotional situation.

At the same time, a metaphor is also an emotional experience because it's evocative. A battlefield is a very emotional place to be! Even though you've moved sideways (thinking about war instead of interpersonal relationships), the metaphor works only because all the emotions—the uncertainty, the anger, the fear, the sadness, the desire to dominate, the desire to retaliate, the desire for peace—are still there and resonate between relationships and battlefields. You haven't left your emotions behind at all! You've just moved them into the imaginative space of the metaphor. The evocativeness of a good metaphor helps you feel your feelings, even as the playfulness of a good metaphor distracts from the intensity of your feelings.

The Goldilocks zone of emotional vulnerability is not too intellectual and not too emotional, but just right. You come away from the

---

17 NASA. (2003, October 2). "The Goldilocks Zone" [Press release].

metaphor with greater understanding, emotional clarity, and the capacity to think about your situation without getting flooded.[18]

Skills for Playing with Metaphors for Greater Clarity and Satisfaction in Life

Discovering/Creating Metaphors

So, where the heck do metaphors come from? How exactly do they come to mind? A few answers:

Discover them in your language.[19]

You cannot speak for long without stumbling over a metaphor. If you describe the situation you'd like to explore and what you'd like to do with it, chances are high that there will be one or more metaphors lurking in your language. Here are some tips for identifying them:

- Look for spatial language, such as *in, on, between, about, through*, etc. Keep an eye out especially for prepositions. Since they describe the relation between two things in a sentence, they are pretty much always spatial. Whether you are deep in love or deep in depression, both love and depression are described as containers in which you find yourself far from the exit.
- Get nerdy. Take some crucial words from your description of the situation/problem, then look up their synonyms or, even nerdier, etymology.[20] You'd be surprised how many words are hiding metaphors in them. One of my favorites is *overwhelm*, which originally meant something like "to turn upside down," "to knock over," or "to submerge completely." Another good one is *struggle*, which is connected to *wrestle* and *grapple*.

---

18 Flooded—a therapeutic water metaphor for emotional intensity, when we feel swept away by emotion, filled with it, drowning in it, etc. Gosh, metaphors are fun.
19 Lakoff, G., & Johnson, M. (1981). *Metaphors We Live By*. University of Chicago Press.
20 https://www.etymonline.com/

Discover them in your body.[21]

Postures, gestures, facial expressions, and even the sensations you feel are all physical expressions of how you feel in and about a situation. By identifying your physical state, you can then ask, "When else is my body in this state?" The answer to that question provides your metaphors.

Some examples: Clenching your fists could signal that you are holding on to something/someone or wanting to attack something/someone. Raised shoulders can indicate a desire to be protected or shrug off a burden. A disgusted facial expression shows that you're treating something/someone like poisonous or odious food.

I don't know!

Honestly, a lot of times, metaphors just seem to pop up. It's a little like asking a writer, "Where do you get your ideas?" Inspiration is like that. You have this deep and mysterious reserve of imagination from which images can arise . . . and I don't quite understand it. Sometimes, creativity just happens to you.

Phil Lesh, former bassist of the Grateful Dead, was known for playing jams in which songs segued into one another, creating one long chain of music. The segue is a type of musical riddle. How do we make a smooth transition from one discrete piece of music to another? When asked one night about how his band would make a particular transition, he remarked, "I'm not really sure. Why don't we just hallucinate a solution as we're playing?"[22] While I am not endorsing hallucinogens,[23] it's a fascinating point that, when we're playing—or noodling around, as it's sometimes called—the next step can make itself known. But we discover it only by playing.

---

21 Gendlin, E. T. (1969). Focusing. Psychotherapy: Theory, Research & Practice, 6(1), 4–15. https://doi.org/10.1037/h0088716
22 Budnick, D. (2020, August 26). Neal Casal: Hallucinating a Solution for Fare Thee Well. Relix. https://relix.com/articles/detail/neal-casal-hallucinating-a-solution-for-fare-thee-well-relix-revisited/
23 Outside of currently professionally acceptable therapeutic settings.

Playing with Metaphors

Once you've got your metaphor, it's time to play with it, extend it, and transform it to make it useful as a lateral space for problem-solving. Here are some ways to do that:

Extension - The metaphor is an image, so picture it fully.

If you're wrestling with something/someone, what position are you each in? Where are you able to grasp the other, and how do you evade the other's attempt to grasp? Which parts of yourself or the other person are the most stable and grounded, and which parts are the most vulnerable?

If you're overwhelmed by something, what is the storm? The boat? The waves? An anchor? Who else is on the boat with you?

If your face is expressing disgust, you're dealing with a food metaphor. What are you being forced to eat, and what about it makes you think it's poisonous or odious?

Extension - The metaphor is a story, so fill out the story.

How did you end up wrestling? Why are you wrestling? Is there a crowd watching, and who are they cheering for? What's the goal? What will happen after the wrestling match?

How did you get on this boat? Where is it supposed to be heading? How long have you been out at sea? What would a skilled sailor do in this situation? How will you recognize when the storm has passed?

Who is offering you this odious food? What's the worst that will happen if you eat it? What would you rather eat instead? What does your hunger and appetite want?

Transformation - The metaphor is part of an overarching category of metaphors, so move your thinking to that overarching level and see what new metaphors are possible. Once you have a new metaphor to play with, expand it out.

Whether your love is like an ocean, a deep well, or a long and winding road, you know one thing—it's a kind of space! Space is an overarching category of metaphors. The different types of spatial metaphors are determined by the boundaries or openings of a space, from entirely closed up (fortresses and traps) to entirely open (abysses and oceans) and everything in between (containers, paths, platforms). Spatial metaphors show up everywhere, as proven by these song titles:

Traps/Fortresses

- "Castles Made of Sand" (Jimi Hendrix)
- "Another Brick in the Wall" (Pink Floyd)
- "Gimme Shelter" (Rolling Stones)

Containers

- "Got to Get You into My Life" (Beatles)
- "Can't Help Falling in Love" (Elvis)
- "Box of Rain" (Grateful Dead)

Paths

- "Life Is a Highway" (Rascal Flatts)
- "End of the Road" (Boyz II Men)
- "Backwards Down the Number Line" (Phish)

Platforms

- "Livin' on the Edge" (Aerosmith)
- "Mama's Always on Stage" (Arrested Development)
- "One Foundation" (Bob Marley)

Abysses/Oceans

- "How Deep Is Your Love?" (Bee Gees)
- "Into the Great Wide Open" (Tom Petty)
- "Head Like a Hole" (Nine Inch Nails)

There are, of course, many more examples, as well as types of space that don't fit into my neat little categories. For example, any song about driving is a combination of container (car) and path (road) metaphors. And what about songs involving hills, mountains, potholes, seashores, and other littoral spaces? What the heck (metaphorically speaking) is a burning ring of fire à la Johnny Cash?

The phenomenon of an overarching metaphor is neat and all, but what value does it bring to personal problem-solving? There are two benefits:

i) Each metaphor has its strengths and weaknesses in helping you with personal reflection and resolution. Recognizing overarching metaphors gives you the power to *change the metaphor you're using*. Someone whose boundaries have been violated may want to lock themselves in a fortress, which is safe . . . but also confining. What if, instead of surrounding themselves with rigid boundaries, they introduce secure doors with secure locks? Now they have the option to give someone the key to their heart, thereby achieving safety but without isolation. If you feel like you're falling endlessly into an abyss . . . you'll need to find or make a platform. By recognizing that you're using a spatial metaphor, you now have the option to try out other spatial metaphors.

ii) By understanding what links these metaphors together—in the case of spatial metaphors, this would be boundaries and openings— you're better at assessing their strengths and weaknesses, and you can generate more ideas about how to solve them.

And there are many more overarching metaphors to work with. If you compare life to a chess match, that opens up the category of games as metaphors. Is there a different type of game that better matches your situation and helps you strategize? If you say you're bonded with someone, now physics and chemistry have been introduced as a metaphor space. What are the strengths and weaknesses of different bonds in science, and which kind (metaphorically) would improve your relationship? If you're feeling overwhelmed and take this to mean you're on a boat in a storm, the overarching category could be travel. Is there a better way to get to your goal besides a boat? Maybe something less impacted by a storm?

Now that you've expanded and/or transformed your metaphor to your situation, there's only one step left . . .

Generating Concrete Solutions by Generating Metaphorical Solutions

At this point, I'll demonstrate the entire process through a personal metaphor from my professional life.

I had a client once with whom I was struggling to make progress. *(Salient metaphors—struggle as wrestling, progress as travel).*

When I described the client to my supervisor, I found that I would, in exasperation, hold out my hands, palms up, sometimes open and sometimes clenched. *(A fighting or wrestling metaphor, expressed as grappling, trying to hold, and failing.)*

When I realized the metaphors in play here, I could then ask myself, *Why am I trying (metaphorically) to hold this client? What makes it so hard to get a grip on them? Where am I even trying to get a grip?* In attempting to answer these questions, I realized I was experiencing the client as slippery.

The word *slippery* is a physics metaphor since it implies things like contact, force, traction, and friction. Yep, that expressed it. I found this client slippery, like they kept slipping from my grasp. I wondered, *Why might they want to be slippery? What are they doing to achieve this slipperiness? What should I do to get a hold of—to gain traction—with them?*

I thought of a few ways one deals with slippery things—drying them off, using adhesive, using surfaces with greater traction. Then I asked myself which one would do.

When I thought about why the client might have preferred to be slippery, their trauma history came to mind. *Aha*, I realized. *They are being slippery as a form of self-protection in order to not be physically or emotionally controlled.* If this was the case, I knew I needed to approach them with respect and care.

This was when the metaphorical answer came to me—oven mitts! Soft, dry, comforting, holding without gripping. I knew this was possibly a way to reduce their slipperiness while still helping them feel safe.

Now that I had my metaphorical answer, I pondered its concrete equivalent. What kind of communication is the metaphorical equivalent of oven mitts? Here's what I thought of: kind words *(soft and comforting)*, a calm presence *(a place where their anger can cool down and I wouldn't be harmed)*, and responses that showed understanding without forcing my agenda onto them *(so they could feel held without feeling gripped too tightly)*.

Conclusion

I know this is a lot. It's very heady stuff. It's odd too. You use metaphors all the time, whether you know it or not. Yet it's another thing to do a deep dive like this to enter a metaphor like entering the wardrobe to Narnia.[24] My final recommendations:

- Manage your expectations when trying any of this out. It's quite possible that all of this is a bit overwhelming, and it'll need time to percolate[25] before it's useful to you.
- Remember that it all comes down to play and imagination. A metaphor is simply a word picture, and you are learning to become a more intentional artist. You may need to make a mess before your vision comes together.
- While it's all quite heady, it's worth it only if you can feel it—if the metaphor pulls at your heartstrings the same way the actual situation does. You'll know a good metaphor because your head

24 Another famous allegory.
25 Coffee metaphor!

starts feeling clearer and your heart feels open and responsive. That's the good stuff.

- You don't have to use this method! And it's not always helpful. Sometimes, you just need to think about the problem head-on or process a situation directly through emotional and somatic[26] therapy.

In the following chapters, I'll share some of my favorite metaphors to use with clients to give you more examples of how this all works and the opportunity to make them your own.

Okay, deep breath. Good luck! And have fun.

---

26 Fancy therapy word for "body-oriented."

"Yes, I know the party is over, but I just can't leave!"

The Guest Who Won't Leave the Party

What Brings up This Metaphor

- Complaining about anxious thoughts that come at night
- Worrying that this means that anxiety is who you are

The Basic Metaphor

Imagine you are hosting a party with a lot of guests. As the night goes on, some folks leave, and others hang around. When the party is ending, there's only one guest left—and it's the annoying one. Being the last guest at the party does *not* mean they are the life of the party! It just means they didn't leave—and probably that they don't know or don't care that they're unwelcome.

When the party was still full, the annoying one was there, but you were engaged with so many good guests, so many people to enjoy, that the annoying guest couldn't really bother you. You weren't distracted. You were engaged! You're here for the other party guests, not for this one. But now this is the only one left. So what do you do with the last annoying guest?

Solving the Metaphor

Say to the last "guest" (the annoyingly persistent voice of anxiety), "Hey, I'm gonna start cleaning up now." If they want to follow you around talking, let them talk. But don't respond—don't give them any conversational fuel. The attitude is: "Okay, fine, they might not go away, but I don't have to engage. I know they're annoying, and so I can keep silent." Or say, "Okay," "Uh huh," and "I see," until they get bored. Maybe they fall silent and leave. If they have something useful or productive to say, it's good to recognize that and respond. Otherwise, no thanks.

The Lesson

Anxiety is useful when it alerts you to a problem, motivating you to find and apply helpful solutions. It's not useful when now is not the time for problem-solving. The anxious voice will do its thing anyhow. "Okay, fine. Do your thing, anxiety. But I don't need to entertain you right now. You might be a piece of who I am. That doesn't make you my core."

The Bread Thief

What Brings up This Metaphor

- Having angry outbursts
- Feeling stuck in anger

The Basic Metaphor

You're starving and holding your last loaf of bread when someone steals and eats it in front of you. How might you respond? The most common answer: Attack the thief! This will hopefully feel emotionally satisfying. But unfortunately, it has no nutritional value.

Solving the Metaphor

It makes sense to attack the thief—you're angry, and they stole your bread. But . . . attacking them doesn't put food in your stomach! It's more important—either now or eventually—to focus on your hunger, not your anger.

You can move past the anger (at least temporarily) by refocusing on the need and how to get it met. If this person or situation is a dead end (the thief cannot return the loaf now that it's eaten), you need to find a different resource, a different way forward. Even if the next step is getting financial restitution from the thief, you should seek it in order to get fed, not to get revenge. It's okay to be hangry,[27] but remember to focus on the hungry part, not just the anger.

The Lesson

Anger is important; it's a natural response to being unable to fulfill a need because a person or situation is in the way. But! When you are focused entirely on anger, you forget its intended function, which is alerting you to the status of a need and motivating you to address it.

---

27 "Hangry" = Hunger + Angry. Oxford University Press. (n.d.) Hangry. *Oxford English dictionary*. Retrieved August 31, 2024 from https://www.oed.com/dictionary/hangry_adj?tab=factsheet#1222708960

The Broken Pinky Toe

What Brings up This Metaphor

- Dismissing your own problems because "others have it worse"
- Believing you "have no right to complain"

The Basic Metaphor

In the summer of 2020, I was seeing clients virtually from my coworker-less office. One time between sessions, I was stepping out from my desk (with a very narrow space between the desk and the wall) and broke my pinky toe in the way (I assume) that all pinky toes get broken—by slamming them into something.

Now then, this is a weird question, but . . . If you had to choose a bone to break, which one would you choose? I'm assuming it's your pinky toe because every other bone would likely hurt even more to break and impact functioning in a worse way. Right? (I'm not a doctor.) So, really, it's just a pinky toe. What's the big deal?

Solving the Metaphor

But . . . Do you think it hurt? My gosh, *so much*. I definitely did a little bit of crying. It really hurt! Yes, I was grateful for my general health and for the fact that it could've been so much worse. But I don't think anyone would fault me for being in distress, even if it was only a little pinky toe. I just shouldn't complain to someone with a broken leg.

The Lesson

Saying, "Others having it worse," doesn't take away your right to feel bad and complain (except maybe not specifically to those people who have it worse than you). If it hurts, it hurts! It's your pain. Dismissing it as too small doesn't make it hurt less. By acknowledging your physical or emotional pain, you have the opportunity to feel self-compassion and take care in whatever way you need it. Your broken pinky toe may be nothing compared to bigger problems, *and* it's still important enough for some medical attention.

"I don't think Nebraska ever ends!"

Driving Through Nebraska

What Brings up This Metaphor

- Going through a hard time
- Worrying that you'll feel this way forever
- Wishing you would grow/heal faster

The Basic Metaphor

So, I've never driven through Nebraska, but here's what I've heard:[28] (1) It takes a really long time—about seven hours. (2) There's a ton of space between towns. And (3) there are *a lot* of cornfields. When I imagine that drive, I imagine driving very fast but seemingly getting nowhere, since the scenery doesn't change much. I'm moving, but am I getting anywhere? Will I ever get to the other side of this state?

Solving the Metaphor

Good news! Of course I will get to the other side. It might take a long time, but with a working car and enough gas, determination, and rest periods, I will get to the other side. I have to keep at it, even if it doesn't look like I'm getting anywhere. Of course, a roadmap, GPS, and maybe a traveling companion are also useful resources.

The Lesson

Progress can be invisible, which is annoying and discouraging. But progress is indeed happening. A plan and a buddy (maybe a therapist?) can help you get through, both logistically and emotionally.

As an aside, there's another metaphor I use that expresses this same sentiment but may appeal more to some folks' imaginations: "Almost every step out of the wilderness will mostly look like more wilderness."

---

28 To give respect to Nebraska, I'll note that my source on this also assures readers that Nebraska has much more to it than cornfields. Wolters, M. (2020, December 16). 10 Things That Will Blow Your Mind about Nebraska. Wolter's World: Honest Travel Advice. https://woltersworld.com/10-things-that-will-blow-your-mind-about-nebraska/

"You have been chewing on that stuff for two hours, are you ever going to swallow it?"

Ruminants and Rumination

What Brings up This Metaphor

- Ruminating (repetitive and unproductive negative thinking/ obsessing)
- Labeling yourself as an overthinker

The Basic Metaphor

What therapists call ruminating is a common symptom of anxiety, but to use this word in this way is a waste of a great metaphor. In zoology, ruminants are a category of animals—including cows, sheep, deer, etc.—that digest their food twice by fermenting it in a foregut, regurgitating, chewing again (a.k.a. chewing the cud), and swallowing again. At this point, the food goes to the true stomach. The cud-chewing part is also called rumination, from the Latin *ruminare*, which means "to chew over again."[29]

So, this means we're all using the word *rumination* incorrectly! What we call rumination is very unproductive for us, but actual ruminating (the animal kind) is *very* productive for those animals. We chew on the same thoughts again and again, getting nowhere. But what if we were to chew again (metaphorically) the way actual ruminants do?

Solving the Metaphor

The core metaphor in play here is processing, which can describe a digestive and/or an emotional process.[30] In productive processing, we break down material, turning it into nutrients to be absorbed or waste products to be excreted.

Awareness of the digestive process, as well as ways of facilitating it, will make our eating experience (and its aftermath) more pleasant and productive. We can target the food effectively by using different types of teeth appropriately, eating and chewing slowly, drinking the right liquids at the right times, resting or moving afterward as needed, and expecting the process to take time.

---

29 Ruminant. (2024, August 31). In Wikipedia. https://en.wikipedia.org/wiki/Ruminant
30 Also a manufacturing process, but I'll leave you to expand and solve that one yourself.

The Lesson

In emotional processing, you can think and feel through your experiences to identify what you've taken in from them, then figure out what to keep and what to let go of. Because your experiences and emotions can be complicated, processing them may not be a one-and-done affair; you may need to chew things over again.

For this to be productive, you may need to use a variety of methods for processing. This can include talking to a friend, using talk and/or experience-based therapies, writing it down, crying it out, turning it into art, turning it into activism, or making new plans and resolutions for addressing it in the future, etc. This kind of ruminating (thinking and rethinking productively) is very helpful as part of a larger process of growing and healing.

Now You Try! Exercises in Metaphorical Musing

A friend recently asked me for advice about something. Here's what they said:

> "So, I am very bad at keeping in touch with people. Every so often, I vow to be better, but I end up getting overwhelmed and continuing my habit of not keeping in touch."

Exercise #1: Spot the Metaphors

Can you identify the metaphorical language in this request for advice?

- Tip #1: Look for nonliteral language. Which words or phrases aren't meant literally?
- Tip #2: Use etymology! Cut and paste any significant words into www.etymology.com and see if the root of the word has a metaphorical meaning.

See below for the answers

EXERCISE #1: ANSWER KEY:

- **Keep in touch:** Since my friend probably doesn't mean actual physical contact, this would be a physics metaphor, relating all social contact to physical contact.
- **Overwhelmed:** Its etymology shows that it's a spatial metaphor, relating an emotional state to a boat being overturned in the water.
- **Continuing:** Its etymology shows that it's also a spatial metaphor, relating the persistence of an action (not keeping in touch) to the act of traveling in a direction.

Exercise #2: Understand the Topic Metaphorically

My friend wants to do better at keeping in touch, and we now understand that they mean social contact, not necessarily physical contact. Use the metaphor of physical contact to explore what kinds of social contact they might mean by drawing lines to match one to another below.

Some Types of Physical Contact	Types of Social Contact
Bumping into	Celebrating together
Pinching	Having an argument
Clashing	Reminding
A shoulder to lean on	Agreement
A shot in the arm	A brief, light interaction
High-fiving	Emotional support
Seeing eye to eye	Encouragement

See below for the answers

EXERCISE #2: ANSWER KEY:

- Bumping into = Brief, light interaction
- Pinching = Reminding
- Clashing = Argument
- A shoulder to lean on = Emotional support
- A shot in the arm = Encouragement
- High-fiving = Celebrating
- Seeing eye to eye = Agreeing

Exercise #3: Understand the Problem Metaphorically

What can make it difficult to stay in touch socially? You might gain some clarity by first exploring what makes it difficult to stay in touch physically. For this next exercise, I challenge you to come up with your own translations of the metaphor.

Some Challenges of Physical Contact	Challenges of Social Contact
My/their hands are slippery.	
One of us is already in contact with someone else.	
How do we know when to stop hugging?	
I went to shake hands; they went to fist-bump.	
My/their hands are literally tied.	
We're stranded on separate islands.	
My/their hands are sticky.	

EXERCISE #3: ANSWER KEY:

Here are some potential answers (yours may vary):

- My/their hands are slippery = Not responding or giving evasive answers to questions
- One of us is already in contact with someone else = Overbooked social calendar
- How do we know when to stop hugging? = How do we know when to stop conversing?
- I went to shake hands; they went to fist-bump. = We are misunderstanding each other's intention in communication.
- My/their hands are literally tied. = Too busy dealing with a personal issue
- We're stranded on separate islands. = Logistical difficulties (No Wi-Fi, language barriers, etc.)
- My/their hands are sticky. = One of us is dealing with a personal matter that they don't want the other to know about or feel burdened by it.

61

Exercise #4: Solve the Problem Metaphorically

Take one of the challenges of physical contact listed previously or come up with your own. If that was the situation, how could you solve it? How could that physical solution be translated into a social solution?

62

YOU HAVE TO LIVE WELL WITH YOUR LIMITATIONS

"I am ignorant of absolute truth. But I am humble before my ignorance and therein lies my honor and my reward."

— Sand and Foam, by Kahlil Gibran

"I never know if I can handle anything. That's what makes my life so exciting!"
— Todd Chavez, Bojack Horseman

You're not sure what to do next. Maybe it's because the next step is unclear. Maybe the next step is very risky. Maybe you knew what the next step was supposed to be, but now something new is in the way. Maybe you don't know if you'll get a chance to try again. Maybe you're not quite sure where you're ultimately heading. Maybe the next step is going to be decided for you, and it's not in your control. Whatever the reason for your uncertainty, it leaves you feeling powerless, uncertain, confused, fearful, embarrassed, or even ashamed.

You're in the forest of limitations, and there are many trees blocking the way.

There are myriad limitations you can encounter in the forest. You might not be able to see the way forward due to fog, dense brush, high walls, faded trail markers, or paths that simply trail off. You might struggle to move forward due to steep climbs, unbridgeable gaps, fallen trees across the path, boulder mazes, and other real or apparent dead ends. You face risks—poisonous plants, dangerous animals, and heights from which to fall. Negotiating the terrain is tiring. In the forest, you learn very quickly that you are not all-powerful.

With each obstruction, challenge, and risk faced, the same questions arise: What's stopping you? What is so difficult about this? Do you have the resources to take it on? Should you push through, take a break, or turn around? Is this as far as you can go?

Take the example of encountering a fallen tree blocking the path. The first thing you'll need to do is stop. Then you consider the relationship between the tree and the path and whether there are any ways to get around it. You consider the relationship between yourself and the tree as well as whether you have the internal strength or external tools to climb or bust through it. You make a few attempts to get over, around, and through. Finally, you consider the relationship between yourself and the path and to what extent you can tolerate obstacles, detours, and dead ends. You may get through, or you may not. And you may make peace with it, or you may not.

There are myriad limitations you can encounter in life. You might run up against your own ignorance, weakness, inability, vulnerability, and mortality. It's dangerous. It's scary. It's discouraging!

With each obstruction, challenge, and risk faced, the same questions arise: What's stopping you? What is so difficult about this? Do you have the resources to take it on? Should you push through, take a break, or turn around? Is this as far as you can go?

Broadly speaking, there are two types of skills required when struggling to make progress on your way—problem-solving and problem-tolerating. Both types require emotional strengths, like patience and self-compassion. Problem-solving requires curiosity about the challenge, ingenuity in using personal and environmental resources, and the ability to generate, weigh, and try out various options. Tolerating a problem requires the ability to pause, reflect, and be open to the possibility of failure.

The essays in this section are meditations on our limitations as individuals, with my recommendations for facing, challenging, and often resigning ourselves to our limitations. If you can develop a greater appreciation for the inevitable reality of your limitations, you'll be better able to face the challenges of life with clear eyes and realistic hopes.

You Are a Limited Person
(And So Am I)

Did you know that you are very limited? I'm not saying this to get you down. I'm sure you are aware, even more than I am, of your limitations. I want to talk about the wisdom of *owning your limitations*. I'll do this by pointing out a number of mine. Hopefully, you will find some of my confessions true for yourself, and they might inspire you to own your unique limitations.

I'm only one person. I have one body, one mind, one location, and one life. That means I can try to have an effect on the world as a whole, but I can't save it alone. That means I can try to support my loved ones, but I can't be their only person. It's hard to be only one person, but since that's not going to change, I need to reshape my hopes and plans to work with this reality of being solo.

I have a particular perspective. Given my particular class, gender, race, orientation, ability, religious heritage, ethnicities, geographical origin, parental upbringing, opportunities, experiences, and interests, I have a unique perspective. But that leaves out many, many others. My worldly observations and values are shaped around these gaps in my awareness and experience. If I am to gain any wider perspective on human life on Earth, I have to learn to listen and put my perspective aside occasionally.

I have particular strengths and weaknesses. I developed many of these strengths at the expense of the weaknesses. Other weaknesses played a key role in my strengths. For example, I think that being short played a formative role in my desire to be intelligent and witty since I wasn't going to be physically big. At least I could have a big personality. Another example: When I was studying philosophy, theology, and therapy, I wasn't studying law, medicine, business, or other trades. I can train for a career; I can't train for every career. The mistakes I've made[31]—including the ones that hurt me and others extensively— have strengthened me as a person, cultivating my sense of selfhood, relationship, and responsibility.

I'm in process. Due to my own bad habits and reluctance to face my limitations, I feel like I got a slow start in becoming a mature adult. And due to my persistent ignorance, resistance, and prejudice, it continues to be slow going. It's hard to grow, and there are so many forms of personal growth to pursue: physical, intellectual, emotional, interpersonal, cultural, professional, social, societal, political, and ecological, to name a few. I can try each day to improve, but for the most part, I will continue to lag in a number of dimensions. And I will even take steps backward at points. My growth as a person is slow, uneven, and often ambiguous. I will continue to make mistakes.

So, yep—I'm limited. It happens. By owning these limitations, I can accept them humbly and even work on them where possible and desirable.

---

31 If I was able to learn from them.

How to Be Good at Being Clueless

Cluelessness is feeling lost. Maybe you feel that something is wrong, but you don't know what it is. Or you know you're supposed to do something, but what (or when, where, how, and why)? We would all rather feel oriented and confident. When we feel clueless, it's easy for that feeling to spiral and become an abyss of uncertainty, paralysis, and self-condemnation.

Is there some way to have productive cluelessness? Here are my recommendations:

Self-Compassion

Ignorance goes hand in hand with being new at anything. You stand uncertain at the crossroads of major life decisions. When you're new and making big decisions, it makes sense to feel lost! Self-compassion involves feeling bad and hating feeling bad while still validating that it makes sense to feel bad. By practicing self-compassion, you can focus on the dilemma itself rather than getting caught up hating yourself for feeling lost. You're already struggling; you don't need someone (a.k.a. you) yelling at you at the same time.

Patience

Cluelessness is the first step toward getting a clue. This chapter started its life as a blank screen. At multiple points in its creation, my progress stalled—and that lack of progress was also part of the process! It's uncomfortable, but if you remain patient and calm, you can give yourself the time and space to wander, stumble, and float toward a clue.

Curiosity

Multiply your questions! Every question is a prompt for more brainstorming and a signpost toward potential answers. If you're lost in the wilderness, it's better to try out various paths, trace and retrace steps, and gain a better sense of your surroundings. Anything is better than just sitting there. Even a question that goes nowhere (a.k.a. a detour) teaches you more about whatever you're dealing with. The more of a map you can put together, the better chances you have of finding a way out.

One practical tip when dealing with questions is to write them down. A long list of questions can be overwhelming, but not as much as a whirling jumble of them (which is what it feels like when you keep them entirely inside your head).

Playful Imagination

Mapping out this confusing wilderness can be helpful, but you also need to think outside the box. Imagination moves your thinking from the actual to the possible (then hopefully back to the actual). Playfulness gains you some bonus energy for creative problem-solving by raising the question: "You know what would be neat?"

Thankfully, you don't need to reinvent playful imagination for adults. That's what makes the Upright Citizens Brigade (UCB) improv manual[32] such an awesome resource! Three main improv principles are:

---

32 Besser, M., Roberts, I., and Walsh, M. (2013). *The Upright Citizens Brigade Comedy Improvisation Manual.* Comedy Council of Nicea.

"Yes and"

In improv, the "Yes and" principle guides scene partners to work with and build upon whatever the other players present to them. In cluelessness, you have to start with that same acknowledgment—"Okay, like it or not, this is my situation."

"If this is true, what else is true?"

In improv, the "If, then" principle promotes further elaboration of the world in the scene. If you're on an alien spaceship, then . . . There are aliens, they have ships, and you've somehow arrived on one. You can ask questions to expand on the story: What are these aliens like? What does their ship do? How did you get here? What do they want from you, etc.? In improv, you can make up whatever answers you like.

In cluelessness, you can similarly expand your sense of your situation through imagination and playfully generating multiple answers (right, wrong, sensical, nonsensical) to any of your questions just to see what happens. What are all the im/possible ways you got into this situation? What kind of world(s) would have this kind of situation? What roles are other people around you playing in the situation? In playing "If, then," you're aiming to brainstorm and try on different ways of thinking rather than nailing down conclusive narratives.

"Finding the game"

In improv, "The game" is what's funny about the scene. Consider the villain/clown Sideshow Bob from *The Simpsons*. He steps on rake after rake, only to have each one smack him in the face.[33] Each individual rake/smack is solid slapstick, but the game of the scene is more abstract:

---

33 Writer Vitti, J. (Writer), and Moore, R. (Director). (1993, October 7). "Cape Fear" (Season 5 Episode 2) [TV series episode.] In J. L. Brooks, M. Groening, A. Jean, M. Reiss, S. Simon (Executive Producers), *The Simpsons*. Gracie Films; Twentieth Century Fox Film Productions.

Neither he (nor we as the audience) sees the next rake coming, *and they just keep on coming.* In UCB theory, players find the game by noticing whatever is unusual—whatever stands out from the norm. In Sideshow Bob's case, the first rake is standard slapstick, but the second one is unusual. And therein lies the game.

In cluelessness, you're not necessarily looking for the unusual but for the salient. What really *matters* to you in your situation? Call this "finding the theme." The theme is what you're getting lost in. Consider a romantic breakup. That's simply a situation, but what is it that matters here?

- "I thought they were The One!"
- "What went wrong?"
- "Why does this keep happening to me?"
- "How long should I wait before moving on?"

And so on. Recognizing the theme can focus your attention and give direction to your exploration.

All these principles lead to similar exploratory actions. Get busy elaborating on your situation, seeking implied facts based on what you already know, and identifying what matters most when you look at your situation. All of these practices keep you active and looking around rather than simply feeling lost.

Beyond these improv techniques, I have one other intervention to offer, which is also based on the notion of fictional scenes: Treat your situation as if you were in a book or TV show. It can be easier to let loose your imagination in a fictional context! Fictional characters *always* have a motivation, justified or not. Fictional characters are free to act in outlandish ways, so brainstorm freely:

- "What would I do in this situation if I had supernatural powers?"
- "What would I do if there were no consequences?"
- "What would I do if I were [insert fictional character here]?"

Critiquing and modifying an unrealistic (or even immoral) idea can get you closer to a good idea—certainly closer than having no idea.

A Concluding Shameless Plug for Therapy

You might be saying to yourself, *Self-compassion, patience, curiosity, and playful imagination— you're asking a lot of me. Honestly, I'm too preoccupied with feeling stressed out about how clueless I feel!*

This is why a second person (quite possibly a therapist) can be such a valuable tool in being clueless productively. As an outsider to your internal situation, the second person isn't tied up in the same knots you are and isn't caught up in hating the situation and/or themselves. This outside vantage point frees them up to offer compassion, model patience and curiosity, and introduce elements of playful imagination into your problem-solving.

However, it's still important for the second person to join you in your cluelessness. No one can help you out of trouble without truly understanding and respecting what makes it so troublesome. This is not to say that someone can help only if they've been in the same situation as you, but the helper needs to be able to (conceptually) stand inside the dilemma with you, look around, and say, "Hoo boy, that's a tough one! Let's see what we can do, yeah?"

A wilderness is a place of danger and even doom; it's also a place for adventure. In the spirit of adventure, cluelessness is just part of the scene.

Silence Is Completely Ambiguous

Looking into a dense fog or darkness, you know only that you don't see anything. What, if anything, is out there in the fog? What, if anything, awaits you in the darkness? You don't know! Your ignorance makes you uneasy, and your mind goes straight to conjuring up potential threats—a habit which has been, evolutionarily speaking, very wise. Erring on the side of fear is an excellent survival technique, specifically when surrounded by mortal dangers.

Nowadays, if you're in a relatively safe environment, this instinct is often less useful or even problematic. The issue is that looking into the darkness, you see only what you're projecting into it. What you see is usually a reflection of what you fear, not information about what's out there.

But let's change the focus from darkness to silence—specifically, the way interpreting silence can get you into trouble in relationships. When you don't hear from someone, you can get scared or annoyed and assume the worst. But actually, just like darkness, *silence is ambiguous*. It can mean anything and nothing.

There's a story that drove this home for me. For the sake of confidentiality, I have changed almost every single detail of the story except for the ones that serve my point.

Some years ago, a client came to me worried about their situation with their ex. They'd broken up about six months earlier and had kept sporadically in touch since then. But now the ex wasn't returning any communications. The client was anxiously wondering what was going on and finding themselves coming up with all sorts of anxious and paranoid stories: *Is my ex mad at me? Why are they ignoring me? Should I reach out again? But what if my reaching out annoys them further?* And on and on.

As their therapist, I wasn't sure what to say. I didn't know what was going on with the ex either! I didn't want to give the client false reassurances or further paranoia. What I ended up saying was, "Silence is ambiguous. If you're not hearing from someone, you can only know one thing: You're not hearing from them. Any stories you have are the ones you generate for yourself, but only the other person knows the real story."

The client struggled with this even while acknowledging that it made sense. Over time, I would repeat this point, and they got better at quieting their overactive and over-interpreting mind.

And one day, the client came in excited and said, "You'll never believe it. I found out what was going on!" Their ex had gone away on a long voyage at sea and lost their cell phone over the side of the boat. Their ex had never seen the phone calls.

So that was the reason for the silence! The client was mostly struck by the fact that, among all the answers their anxious mind had constructed, the correct one had been off their radar—they would *never* have guessed it. The client was very glad they'd stopped driving themselves crazy trying to figure it out.

Because silence in communication is ambiguous, you have to be careful not to fill that silence with your own interpretations. Although all you want is an answer, you have to avoid coming to any conclusions because you *just. Don't. Know.*

This is a very hard thing to practice. You can't help but wonder what's going on, and your mind keeps coming up with stories, seeing things in the dark, and hearing something in the silence. Your primal ancestors survived by hearing things in the silence. Your brain is evolutionarily chosen to be a prediction-making machine.[34] And yet, in the

34 Clark. A. (2023). *The Experience Machine: How Our Minds Predict and Shape Reality.* Pantheon.

complications of modern life and communication, it can be beneficial to you and your relationships to, on certain occasions, suspend this incessant predicting and storytelling.

It takes mindfulness. First, recognize that your mind is obsessing and generating stories. Then, realize that your mind is doing so because it otherwise has no idea what's going on. Finally, engage in some compassionate self-talk: "I hate not knowing what's going on! It makes me anxious. I wish I knew. But I don't. And until I get the actual answer, I know I'm gonna keep making them up myself. That makes sense. But I shouldn't get too lost in any of these stories I'm making up. I have to return to letting myself not know. Over and over again, I need to choose the discomfort of not knowing over the anxiety of obsessive storytelling."

The Walled and Welcoming City: A Parable About Emotionally Secure Vulnerability

Somewhere, there's a city that is both walled and welcoming.

Why Is It Walled?

The wall gives the city a sense of identity. Residents know who they are by looking around and seeing what's inside or outside the wall. By containing and abiding all the differences among inhabitants, the wall creates a feeling of unity.

Also, the wall slows or stops anything outside that's trying to enter the city, which creates a sense of boundaries and order. Outsiders can enter the city, but not from just any direction and not all at once. Attackers can also enter the city, but only if they're sufficiently strong. Spears may make it through; tomatoes do not.

If It's Walled, What Makes It Welcoming?

Despite the wall, the city is welcoming in three ways:

1. There are established holes in the wall, a.k.a. gates, for entrance. Outsiders are welcomed in and invited to join as long as they can be good guests.

2. If outsiders are acceptable to the inhabitants, the walls can be expanded to include them.
3. But here's the special detail: Any gaps or weaknesses in the wall are not defended. Instead, any attacker that makes it through is met by a welcoming committee.

Wait, What? There's a Welcoming Committee?

These are citizens who know where all the weak points are because they like to know as much as possible about the city. It's how they express their love—they study the city and always want to learn more. One of their favorite ways to learn more is to examine the attackers who are savvy enough to find the gaps and strong enough to get through them. Because of their curiosity, the welcoming committee is much more interested in understanding these threats than just reacting defensively against them.

The welcoming committee is composed of engineers, human resources representatives, and members of the city think tank.

The engineers want to learn more so they can better reinforce the walls. They know there will always be more gaps, but they're still interested in addressing the weaknesses that come up.

The human resources folks want to understand the attackers better and perhaps find a way they can become part of the city. Who knows? Whatever makes its way inside may be important to hold on to!

The think tank members want to learn so they can better understand, appreciate, and even preserve the city's idiosyncrasies. They're not sure whether and what they'll do with the knowledge, but they're always curious just in case new information helps them figure something out later.

Why Doesn't Anyone Feel Threatened by the Attackers?

The city is arranged so it can have weaknesses without having insecurity. What's the difference? A weakness is an unintended point of entry; an insecurity is something that threatens the city's existence and essence.

But what is the essence of this particular city? What if this welcoming committee, a group of concerned citizens who are fascinated by critical feedback, is also the essence? If that's the case, attacks are quite welcome! If the city had a rigid order—an obsession with the status quo—these attacks would be very threatening.

No one feels threatened because the citizens love the city as something that changes and as an organism that is always in need of growth and repairs. They thrive by serving it however they can. If an attacker were to bring down some section of the city, the citizenry would cheerfully continue its work, seeing the destruction as the start of a new and exciting municipal project. The citizens don't feel overwhelmed by a big project because they love working even more than they love completing the work. The citizen-builders don't lose heart because they feel comfortable anywhere. They can take their rest, relaxation, and recreation even in the midst of a big project. In fact, when there are no outside attackers, the citizens will try to pick apart the wall themselves just to see what happens.

If every attacker is seen as a chance for enrichment, they see no need to get defensive.

Shouldn't a Parable Have More Drama?

Probably! A good story requires drama, and drama is generally fueled by insecurity. A walled and welcoming city will have far less drama than a desperately guarded fortress. So, sorry! And . . . see the next chapter for the translation of this parable.

The Best Defense Is a Good Sense of Self: An Explanation of the Walled and Welcoming City

Weakness Is Built into Being Human

Because no one is perfect, all-knowing, or all-powerful,[35] each of us has areas of relative powerlessness and various weaknesses, and this means we can't avoid having personal problems. If you were all-powerful, you would never need to worry about the things that are partially or completely out of your control. This is typical stuff, like your appearance, skills or lack thereof (a.k.a. mediocrity), ignorance, and decisions, as well as other life challenges, like traffic, illness, and whether others will say yes to you. If you simply had the power to change these things, you would have no need to learn to deal with having limitations.

In order to ground this chapter in the real world, I'll need to confess a personal limitation: I don't know how to change a tire on either my bike or my car.

Approaches to Limitations

So, what can I do with my various limitations? I see three approaches:

---

35 Unless your religion says otherwise, in which case interpret "no one" as "no mere human."

1. I can **tolerate** a limitation, let it be as it is, and allow myself *not* to work on it. Taking a tolerant approach, I will continue not to know how to change a tire.
2. I can **make an effort**, aiming to improve myself and overcome this limitation. Making an effortful approach, I will take steps to learn how to change a tire.
3. I can **be indecisive** and not sure whether I will ultimately tolerate or work on overcoming this limitation. Continuing with an indecisive approach, I will bounce back and forth between caring and not caring about learning how to change a tire.

Attitudes <u>About</u> Limitations

I'm calling tolerance, effort, and indecision approaches because they pertain to the actions we take (or not) when we have to deal with a personal limitation. Approaches are about actions. I want to differentiate them from attitudes, which I'm defining here as an emotional state with regard to a problem, regardless of approach. What you might *feel* about these weaknesses is distinct from what you can *do* about them. I see two main attitudes:

1. You can feel **insecure** about it. It makes you anxious to think about it. You avoid situations that will bring it up. If a person or situation reminds you of your limitation, you'll react defensively. In regard to tires, I can tell I'm insecure when the tire pressure light comes on and I'm hit with pangs of shame and inadequacy.
2. You can be **at peace** with it. You face the problem without anxiety, calmly, and with ownership ("To be responsible for something; to embrace and exhibit something about oneself with confidence").[36] I'm still working on that one in regard to tires. In the section below, I'll elaborate more on what being at peace can sound like.

---

36 thefreedictionary.com, s.v., "own it," accessed March 17, 2024, https://idioms.thefree dictionary.com/own+it

It's All About Attitudes

No matter what your approach to a problem is, you can feel insecure or at peace about that approach. I can feel insecure or at peace about changing tires, whether I'm tolerating it, working on it, or conflicted about it. It's the attitude that shapes my mood and experience.

Approaches and Attitudes About Not Knowing How to Change a Tire

	Insecure	*At Peace*
Tolerating	"I guess I'm just giving up; I'm resigning myself to failure."	"I don't have enough time, patience, interest, or hope to learn every life skill. So, while I would rather not have this problem, I'm okay with not working on it."
Working on it	"It's so embarrassing that I haven't learned this yet."	"At least I'm trying, which is both scary and promising. It's humbling—but not humiliating—to be struggling with this."
Conflicted about it	"Why am I so wishy-washy?"	"I'm still conflicted about what to do! I'd rather have a plan, but my confusion and uncertainty are just *where I'm at right now.*"

Secure Vulnerability

Now that I've established my various terms and categories, here's the payoff:

When you are at peace with any of your limitations, you have the capacity for secure vulnerability. When other mental professionals talk about it, secure vulnerability involves trust and courage—the trust you feel in the context of a secure relationship and the courage needed to share your weaknesses even at the risk of being hurt. But I'm describing a secure vulnerability that requires neither trust nor courage because *there's no emotional risk involved.* When you're at peace, you can be vulnerable (open about yourself) without feeling vulnerable (open to injury).

If secure vulnerability doesn't require trust or courage, what does it require?

It requires a solid sense of self—a state that is built upon these traits:

Self-compassion	"I'm human, and everyone has their strengths and weaknesses. It's okay not to be perfect at everything."
Self-critique without self-condemnation	"There are a lot of things I'm not good at yet and others that are fully out of my control; that doesn't mean I'm a failure or worthless."
Process orientation	"At my best, I'm always a work in progress. It's okay to feel clueless, uncertain, conflicted, and trying to figure it out."[37]

These traits are all combinations of two seemingly incompatible attitudes: confidence and humility. Weird, right? You have to know what you're good at, then feel good about that. You have to know what you struggle with, then be nice to yourself about it. The right combination of confidence and humility is essential in having a solid sense of self—one neither overinflated by pride nor crushed by shame.

The Benefits of Secure Vulnerability

When you're at peace with your weaknesses (regardless of how you approach them), you won't get defensive when someone brings it up. With this kind of internal security, you have the freedom to be open

---

37 Wittels, H. [Twitter handle]. (2014, May 20). Also let's stop finding a new witch of the week and burning them at the stake. We are all horrible and wonderful and figuring it out. [Tweet]. Retrieved from https://twitter.com/twittels/status/468880373523689472?lang=en

and vulnerable whether or not you're in a safe space. You won't have aggressive or submissive reactions to criticism; instead, you can be nonreactive, saying things like:

- "That's interesting. I want to think about that."
- "I know."
- "Yeah, it's something I'm still working on."

Being at peace with a weakness also frees you up to discuss it with others. You can use this power to disarm others. If you're open about and at peace with your issues, what can you be attacked with? Where's your need for armor or weapons when your safety is assured from within?

Even more powerfully, being at peace with a weakness frees you up to recruit others if you're looking to resolve a conflict or work on a problem. Without shame, there's no need to hide. You can ask for help from friends, family, coworkers, and therapists (or a car mechanic).

Conclusion: Even This Essay Has Its Weaknesses

It's okay to critique this! It's a work in progress, just as I always am. I feel pretty good about these ideas, but I'm open to pushback. I won't be surprised or ashamed if someone shows me how I'm not seeing the bigger picture. I've got nothing to defend, and I'm excited to work on myself.

IF YOU'RE HAPPY
AND YOU KNOW IT . . .
YOU'VE GOT OPTIONS

"It starts with being willing to feel what we are going through."

— Pema Chodron

"Emotions are messy and hard to figure out."

— Spike Jonze

You're feeling disturbed. Something big or small has shifted in your world, and now you're feeling those changes inside yourself. It doesn't feel right, and everything felt fine before! New feelings take root, growing within you, and it feels like they are taking over. What happens next? Is this the new normal? What happened to the old you? Who will the new you be?

You're in the forest of emotions.

The life cycle of a forest is defined by disturbances and successions. Disturbances are events that change the ecosystem. They can be as small as a single tree falling down or as large as fires, landslides, meteors, outbreaks, grazing, trampling, war, pollution, and invasive species. Succession is the process by which species in the forest recover and regenerate after a disturbance.

Most disturbances are not threats to the forest—they are simply part of its life cycle. A disturbance that fells trees creates openings for other life to grow. Recovery and regeneration follow, which can be a chaotic process, with various species competing for space and light. One species of tree may shoot up and take over the canopy, blocking out the light needed by species in the understory (the forest floor). An invasive species can pop up and take over, preventing the natives from returning. In either of these scenarios, the lack of diversity in this stage of forest life may lead to another disturbance—the ecosystem collapsing without mutual support between the species. When species cooperate, the forest has a better chance of stabilizing (until, of course, the next outside disturbance).

As humans and stewards of the environment, we need to be sensitive to the forest's life cycle. We shouldn't try to prevent all disturbances. In the aftermath of a disturbance, we shouldn't rush in to fix it all. Rather, we should monitor the forest's responses and work alongside its own process of recovery. While it appears chaotic, the forest is not a mess. It's going through its natural processes. We should honor how the life of the forest is itself a constant conversation among its species and their needs. We should be careful about what new species take root and be responsive to invasion. A forest consumed by one species will not last.

An individual's emotional life is defined by needs, efforts to meet those needs, and the inner and outer events that impact those needs and efforts. While you might prefer to experience only happiness and stability (of your needs being met), your life is defined by its disturbances and how you recover and grow following them. After a disturbance, you might feel like a mess, but it's more complicated than that. Observe how your various needs, actions, and emotions take their time in responding to the change and see what works with the new normal. Don't try to prevent all disturbances. And don't rush in to fix everything or insist on an old and rigid normal. Impulsive actions may feel like they are taking care of your emotional distress, but they don't necessarily stabilize your system. Emotions that completely take over are dangerous to the whole; you'll be healthier if you cultivate layers of emotion, excluding nothing and allowing each its appropriate place in your emotional ecosystem.

The essays in this section will explore various emotions, how each one is an expression of a need, how they compete for space, and how you can nurture each one within the larger whole of your inner life. By recognizing and honoring how your emotions compete and cooperate, you will have more options for managing them and optimizing how you survive and thrive.

Despair Is Part
of the Process

I'm a student during finals. I've done all the reading, and now I'm sitting at the computer. There's nothing left but to write the damn essay. I stare at the blank screen, and I . . . go blank. I get discouraged, and it's an intense feeling. The longer I feel discouraged, the closer I get to giving up. Despair! I don't know where to start, and I'm ready to give up!

But . . . if I don't walk away from the computer (or go clicking around online) . . . if I putter around with my thoughts and ideas . . . if I start jotting down random ideas without the need to put them in order . . . I actually do get started! The essay starts to take shape, and I'm on a roll . . . until I hit some new block or setback. Again—despair! I don't know what comes next!

Can you relate? (If you can relate, sorry for the flashback.)

But here's my move: Staring at the blank screen or the blank line, I use my mantra, "Despair is part of the process." With this mantra, I can recover from discouragement, have patience for the awkward and slow nature of creative work, and trust that I'll gain forward momentum if I keep at it. Because of this mantra, I've learned to anticipate discouragement and despair and to include them in my plan. I also plan for the kinds of responses that might help me—sitting with my mind wandering about the work, brainstorming, taking a short break,[38] or just forging ahead to see what happens.

---

38 With emphasis on the word *short*. At a certain point, a long break is just avoidance.

I tell my clients, "In a ten-step process, despair might be steps 2, 4, and 9."

And so it is with any undertaking an adventure. In any adventure, you want to move forward. Thankfully, there can be smooth, clear, pleasantly downhill parts of the journey, which you find rather enjoyable and encouraging. But if it's really going to be an adventure, there will be sections that are rough, confusing, and uphill. You should expect to feel discouraged.

Discouragement is part of the process. It can be a useful emotion; it causes you to pause and consider what you're up to, where you think you're going, whether it's a worthwhile destination, and whether you're going about it in an effective way. If you're feeling discouraged and doubtful, congrats! You're definitely on an adventure.

The challenge is to keep doubt and discouragement from turning into panic and despair. What's the difference? Consider how when you're on an adventure, you're primarily concerned with orientation (where you are and where you are going) and progress (whether and how you are getting where you want to be).

The difference between doubt and panic relates to challenges in orientation: When you doubt, you stare into the abyss and go blank. When you panic, you fall headlong into the abyss.

The difference between discouragement and despair relates to challenges in progress: When you're discouraged, you get stalled in the mud. When you despair, you lie down in the mud.

Here's a weird endorsement: I know despair isn't great, but if you have to choose between panic and despair, I recommend despair. If you fall into an abyss (a.k.a. panic), it's *very* hard to get out. Even if you do manage to escape after panicking, you're likely to avoid whatever challenge tripped you up in the first place. Since panic disorder is defined by fear of future panic, folks who struggle with panic will do whatever it takes to avoid further exposure to whatever caused their panic, which ends up greatly limiting their options.

But if you lie down in the mud, you'll get dirtier, and it'll be hard to get up, but . . . maybe getting dirty is fine. Maybe a temporary dirt nap is just the kind of rest you need before continuing to slog through the muddy path. Maybe lying down in the mud is just part of the process! Maybe it's okay to feel despair for a little while. It gives you a break from trying and a chance to let your mind wander as you develop new motivations and strategies.

So, if you're working on something hard and you feel slow/stopped/blank, there's no need to feel ashamed. Think to yourself, *Oh right, this is that part where I can't figure out what to do next and start to feel discouragement and despair. It's just a part of the overall thing.* If despair is just a middle step in the process, you can expect and prepare for it and get to the other side of it (soon enough!).

Do You Care Too Much?
Embrace Tiredness!

You are defined by the way you care.[39] What are you besides all those people/places/things you give your time, energy, love, money and attention to? Your emotions and what triggers them are reflections of your care. Even if you're doing something you don't care for (like standing in line at the grocery store), you're doing it for something you do care about (in this case, sustenance).

And yet, when you feel burned out, run-down, and overstressed, you might find yourself saying, "I wish I didn't care so much!" It makes sense—you feel like you're suffering from too much care. Your capacity for care, which is very human, is in overdrive! You're ruminating, you can't sleep, you can't concentrate, and your worry and frustration (emotional responses to care) are overwhelming you. Does this sound accurate? So, of course, if the problem is caring too much, the obvious solution is to care a lot less or not at all, right?

Except—because your care is important and authentic, because you define yourself and find meaning in the realm of care—apathy isn't a realistic or sustainable option. I suggest that, instead of balancing care with apathy, you balance it by embracing tiredness.

This makes a lot of sense on a psychological level. According to Maslow's hierarchy of needs, you are free and able to pursue your higher

39 This is something I picked up in a college course on Martin Heidegger, a groundbreaking existential thinker, though unfortunately also a Third Reich Nazi (and, in my opinion, a terrible writer).

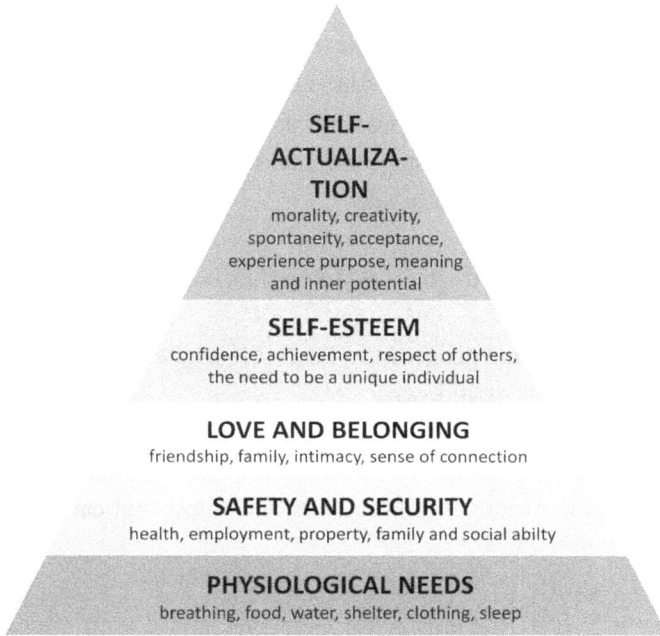

SELF-ACTUALIZA-TION
morality, creativity, spontaneity, acceptance, experience purpose, meaning and inner potential

SELF-ESTEEM
confidence, achievement, respect of others, the need to be a unique individual

LOVE AND BELONGING
friendship, family, intimacy, sense of connection

SAFETY AND SECURITY
health, employment, property, family and social abilty

PHYSIOLOGICAL NEEDS
breathing, food, water, shelter, clothing, sleep

cares (many of which fit in the belonging, love, esteem, and actualization levels of the hierarchy) only when your physiological needs—your more basic cares—are secure. You can't perform as well when you're tired. You ache, you yawn, your head feels heavy, and your limbs feel like lead!

So here's the good news about feeling awful: Because burnout affects you on a physical level, it can serve as a helpful sign that you need to return to attending to your physical needs. But how do you tone down your mental, emotional, and behavioral caring activities, specifically in the spirit of tiredness instead of apathy?

First, identify and honor your passions: "I'm glad that I care about this so much. This is what I value. It's what I hold sacred, and I want to take care of it."

Next, honor your tiredness: "I care deeply but . . . ya know . . . I'm *also* really tired!" This "also" is the key piece here: You're not done caring. It's just that you have other feelings in addition to care. Specifically, you feel tired.

91

Finally, recognize that your passions and tiredness are both essential to living your best life. You'll need to say, "If I want to do my best in caring about this, I'm going to need to take breaks. The only way to make this path sustainable is by maintaining basic upkeep of my body-mind."[40]

Here are some practical steps to make sure that your caring self feels comfortable about taking a break:

1. Ask permission: "I'm glad I'm doing this, but I need a break. Is that okay?"
2. Take note of your progress so far (with whatever you're working on). Literally write it down.
3. Write this down as well: when, where, and how you'll pick up your cares again. Hopefully, in this manner, the caring self can trust that you won't abandon it, and that trust will allow that caring part[41] of you to step back.

If you want to have the energy for the work, guard your energy! You can use your computer only if you regularly charge it. Keep caring but keep maintaining (and appreciating and savoring) those practices that honor the limitations of your energy.

---

40 The term *body-mind* is taken from Maté, G., & Maté, D. (2022). *The Myth of Normal: Trauma, Illness & Healing in a Toxic Culture*. New York, Avery, an imprint of Penguin Random House.

41 Schwartz, R. C., & Sweezy, M. (2020). *Internal Family Systems Therapy* (2nd ed.). The Guilford Press.

Trusting the Anger but Not the Impulse

Every emotion has its purpose: to provide information that can motivate action. Sadness tells you that you've suffered a loss, and its low-energy state leads you to slow down, pause, and face the loss. Fear tells you that one or more of your needs are threatened, leading you to take steps (including freezing in certain types of danger) to protect that need. Anger tells you that someone or something is standing in your way of getting a need met, and its high-energy state leads you to make attempts to overcome that obstacle.

But I noticed something about anger: It's important to trust anger but dangerous to act on it immediately. This is very annoying! Your anger wants you to deal with the problem *now*. But dealing with it right now means doing so while still being angry, which can easily lead to acting impulsively and often in a way that you later regret.

This annoying dynamic is the root of two different types of anger problems. The first, more obvious one, occurs when someone acts rashly when angry. The second, while perhaps better, is still an anger problem. It's when someone is so afraid of acting on impulse that they prefer to convince themselves it's not a big deal, they're not really angry, or they shouldn't be angry. They might be motivated to adopt this conclusion after having an angry and regrettable outburst. They can't trust the impulse anymore, then conclude they need to stop trusting the emotion as well.

The wise way to trust your anger while distrusting your angry impulses is counterintuitive and, therefore, very hard to develop as a habit. The wise way is to *feel the anger but then retreat* in order to:

1. Not express it in its full intensity.
2. Take time to recognize the reason(s) for the anger and the thwarted needs caught up in it.
3. Remind yourself why you'd want to have a nonexplosive relationship with whatever/whoever provoked the anger.
4. Think about when and how you'd like to return and deal with the situation.

The steps require *so* much more carefulness than just yelling or acting out! These steps almost never come to mind in periods of peak anger. In my experience, I usually remember them in the regret phase that follows impulsive anger.

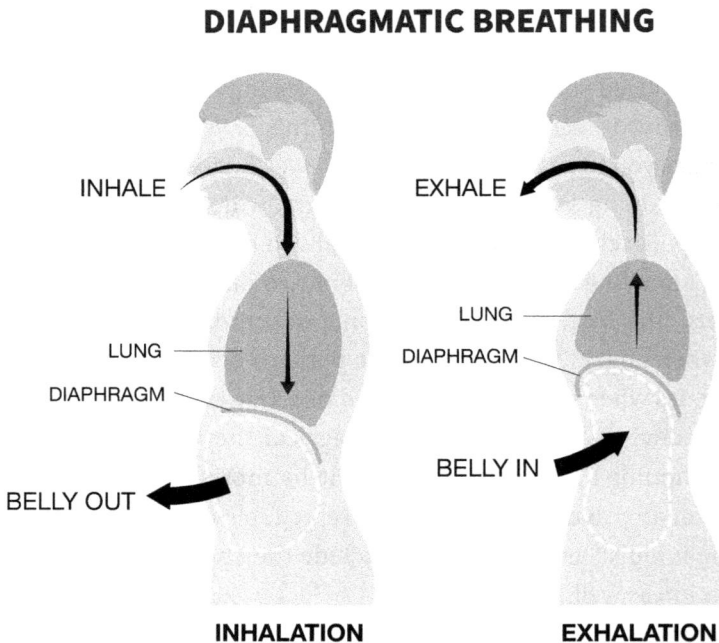

DIAPHRAGMATIC BREATHING

INHALE

EXHALE

LUNG

LUNG

DIAPHRAGM

DIAPHRAGM

BELLY OUT

BELLY IN

INHALATION

EXHALATION

*Inhaling is initiated by expanding the diaphragm and
exhaling is initiated by contracting the diaphragm*

So far, I've found only one way to take these steps,[42] and it takes practice. Work to gain greater awareness of what your anger feels like in your body so that, when you feel physically and emotionally overheated, you can switch your focus away from why you're angry and toward your desire to feel calmer. Try to mindfully observe those bodily states (flushed face, tight jaw, unrest, etc.) that can turn anger into aggression, then maybe make some physical adjustments (breathing diaphragmatically, shifting your posture, rolling your shoulders, etc.) to reduce your tension. It's harder to be as angry when your body is not as worked up.

It's okay if you're unable to completely prevent an angry outburst. In fact, take some pride if you can recognize and interrupt the outburst while it's happening. The sooner you're able to notice and address the physical aspects of anger, the sooner you can remember to pull back and reflect more before taking action. (For more, see "How to Remember to Do That Thing That Made Sense in Therapy" on page 201.) It's a very powerful and mature act to say to yourself (and perhaps the other person), "Oh, I'm getting worked up, and this isn't helping. I'd like to take some time to reflect on this. I'm still angry, but I want to do this right."

It's not easy, and it takes work! I'll leave you with these words of wisdom:

"I can feel your anger. It gives you focus, makes you stronger."

— Emperor Palpatine, Revenge of the Sith

"Don't drive angry!"

— Phil, Groundhog Day

---

42 Well, two ways. Professionally speaking, the right mood stabilizer can also be *very* helpful for managing impulsive anger. (A mood stabilizer is a kind of psychiatric medication used to treat mental health disorders characterized by intense mood shifts.)

How to Have a Good Cry (And Avoid a Bad Cry)

A lot of people don't want to cry, and I get it: When crying, you lose composure, your feeling of self-containment, and the dignity of keeping it together. But not all kinds of crying are created equal!

What Does a Good Cry Feel Like?

A good cry is like a good sneeze (or other bodily functions, but let's keep it classy).

After a good cry, you feel relieved: "Oh man, I needed that!" You had been full of emotion and emotional energy, and the crying provided a way to express and release that emotionality. A good cry might build into a big cry, but it always subsides, leaving a feeling of peace. For cries like this, it's worth letting it all out because afterward, you feel more self-contained and less like you're gonna burst. A good cry can be messy, but you'll feel like less of a mess afterward.

What Does a Bad Cry Feel Like?

A bad cry is one that spirals, comes in waves, and gets worse and worse. At the end, you feel exhausted and empty. Paradoxically, you feel even more full of emotion afterward despite letting it all out.

How Does Each Kind of Cry Happen?

A good cry is infused with self-love. In a good cry, you don't like the situation, but you still like yourself: "Even though I'm sad, I'm still here for me. I don't like feeling this way, but it makes sense to feel this way." In a good cry, you feel the emotion but keep an eye on your body and take steps to down-regulate the physical intensity of your distress. This often includes slower diaphragmatic breathing (using your belly instead of your chest to draw air in and out, as shown on page 94) and/or a comforting self-touch (like resting your hand gently on your chest). Saying one of the above sentiments aloud is also a physical intervention. Speaking makes it more difficult for your thoughts to race, and it gives you a chance to hear someone say something supportive to you.

A bad cry is infused with rejection of self, the situation, and your feeling about the situation: "I shouldn't feel this way. It's so stupid to feel this way. I hate this situation, and I hate feeling bad! I did this to myself." Do you see how these sentiments create a spiral? You hate the situation and yourself for being in it, then yourself for hating yourself for being in it, and so on. The upset multiplies, and so does the intensity of your crying. When you're upset and then get upset that you're upset, your distress gets dug deeper and deeper.

Thoughts related to time can also impact whether you have a good or a bad cry. In a bad cry, you usually make negative and absolute predictions about the future: "This is awful, and it will always be awful!" Some people find it helpful to think, *This too shall pass*. But personally and professionally, I avoid making predictions about the future. For me, saying, "This is hard, but I'm here for me *right now*," works just as well.

Brief Summary of Recommendations

How do you gain more power over which kind of cry you have? As a cognitive behavioral therapist, my recommendations are predictably all about maintaining helpful thoughts and actions. A summary:

Thoughts

- Set an intention: "I'm feeling so much! I think I need a good cry."
- Infuse it with self-love: "I'm sad, but that's because I love myself and feel bad for myself when my needs aren't met."
- Acknowledge feeling bad: "I hate this, and it's okay to hate this."
- Notice and prevent a spiral: "This situation is bad, and I know I hate it. But losing myself in that hate seems to be making this worse. I want to pull back a bit."

Behaviors

- Say the above statements aloud in a comforting (firm but quiet) voice.
- Take slow, diaphragmatic breaths (pulling in air by pushing out the belly).
- Engage in slow, steady touch or movement—something stimulating but not too agitating. Some examples: Take a stroll, brush your hair, stretch, doodle, do domestic cleaning—anything as long as it's done in a slow, calm manner.
- Put on soothing music—not mournful but also not overly cheery.

Conclusion

To use a cliche about the whole thing, I'll say that a good cry happens when your inner parent takes care of your inner child. Part of you needs to cry, and another part is there, ready to hold you while you cry. That's the core intention needed here—to value the crying, value yourself while crying, and simply be there for yourself. There's nothing like a good cry in the arms of someone you feel safe with. If someone else can provide that, great. But it's empowering to be able to provide that for yourself.

I wish for you only to have good cries (but very few reasons to cry).

Want to Move On After a Breakup? Be Disappointed.

Breakups can stir up powerful negative emotions, and two of these emotions can make it difficult to move on—sadness and anger. Both are important emotions, and the sadness and (when appropriate) anger stages should not be skipped! If you lost an important relationship, sadness is appropriate. If you wish it weren't lost and feel like it's someone's (theirs or yours) fault, anger makes sense. But it's easy to get stuck in these feelings. You can be captivated by sadness ("How can I go on?") and anger ("How dare they!").

Let's understand how these two emotions work by framing all emotions as internal responses to how your needs are being met or not. When it comes to relationships, your needs may include things like companionship, recognition, encouragement, affection, physical contact, love, etc. Because these are social needs, you depend on others to fulfill them.

Sadness is a response to losing an important source of need fulfillment. Anger is a response to someone who threatens you or denies you an important source of your needs fulfillment. In the case of a bitter breakup, your ex can be both the lost resource (thus, sadness) and/or the current threat to that resource. You might experience them as withholding, so the anger is your protest and an attempt to restore the ex as a reliable resource for you.

While both sadness and anger are related to your needs, they can become all-consuming and counterproductive. Instead of focusing on your needs, now you're just focused on these reactive emotions! And that's how you get stuck. You lost something important, so you're sad about it, which keeps you focused on the loss, which keeps you feeling sad. Or something was taken from you, and you're angry about it, which keeps you focused on the unfairness of it all, which keeps you angry.

This is where disappointment can serve as a crucial turning point in processing the breakup. By being disappointed in your ex, you integrate (1) sadness about the loss; (2) anger at their role in the loss; but also (3) giving up on seeing them as a reliable resource. That last item is an expression of disappointment. When you become disappointed, you can start to see your ex more fully—as an unalluring package deal and a previously promising relationship that lost its promise. When you become disappointed, it will be easier to stop wanting the relationship back. It's harder to long for a relationship that can't deliver.

Once you're disappointed and no longer see any future promise in the relationship, you're able to return to the primary orientation— getting your needs met. Of course, this can come with a new set of emotions, specifically anxiety and fear. If the last promising relationship was a disappointment, who's to say any future one will deliver? But in this case, at least, you've become desire-oriented and future-oriented, which means you've started to move on.

Additional Note: Moving on from Anger at Yourself

I mentioned in the introduction that, instead of blaming your ex (or *only* blaming your ex), you might feel angry at yourself for the breakup. Being stuck in anger at yourself usually leads to beating yourself up, which creates its own loop of moving back and forth between being angry at yourself and punishing yourself.

In this situation, disappointment in yourself can still be a liberating emotion, although it weirdly works in a way opposite to disappointment in your ex. When you're disappointed in your ex, you give up on them as a resource for your needs. When you're disappointed in yourself, you might feel like giving up on yourself . . . but even so, you can't move on because you will continue to be there with yourself.

However, disappointment in yourself sends the message that you haven't lived up to your own standards and expectations. So, it can serve as motivation to reconsider how you go about taking care of yourself. You can be sad about the loss and angry at your role in it, but the disappointment can motivate you to explore and take steps to do better.

Unconditional Love Is Rarely Appropriate

While it may sound harsh, in my view, there are only two types of human-to-human relationship that call for unconditional love:

1. Parent → child (but not the reverse)
2. Self

I'll elaborate on those, but first, I'll name the relationships I see as inappropriate settings for unconditional love:

1. Partnership and any other kind of friendship
2. Child → parent

Friend Relationships Should Be Conditional

I love my partner very much. And yet, how did I end up with this particular partner? Well, I chose her (and she chose me) from a wide variety of potential partners. How did we make these choices? We based them on particular *conditions*—because the other enjoys particular activities, discusses particular topics, thinks and shares their thoughts in particular ways, etc., etc. If many of those traits were to change radically, I wouldn't love her anymore because I fell in love with a particular person!

I'm sharing this opinion because unconditional love can easily be the setting for abusive relationships. "I love them no matter how they treat me," is one expression of unconditional love, and it's a dangerous one.

Child → Parent Relationships Should Be Conditional

To quote Ayn Rand, "To say 'I love you,' one must first be able to say the 'I.'"[43] The child → parent relationship begins[44] before the child can (literally and figuratively) say "I." The parents are caretakers, attachment figures, security objects, and other roles like that. These foundational relationships exist before the child can see themselves (and their parent) as a full person. They see their parents only as a way of getting needs met.

The early child → parent relationship is, by design, asymmetrical or, at least, transactional in an asymmetrical manner. Here's the deal the child implicitly makes: "You give me love in the form of material and emotional support. In return, I feel attached to you. If you don't give me those things, I won't feel attached." We don't feel much love for the absentee parent, and why should we? This is all *very* conditional.

Once the child becomes an adult, the relationship can get on more equal footing. And yet, the child's love for the parent will still reflect that original asymmetry. Adult love for parents is fueled by past and current feelings of "They have been and/or are there for me." An adult's desire to be there for their parents is built atop that sentiment. The love is not unconditional.

Parent → Child Relationships Should Be Unconditional

First, a disclaimer: This statement is prescriptive ("What should be"), not descriptive ("How things are"). There are indeed parents who love their children only conditionally. (In my work as a psychotherapist, I meet a lot of their children.) But my focus here is on the basis of unconditional love from parent to child.

---

43 Ayn Rand was a twentieth-century writer whose work inspired the modern Libertarian movement. While I'm not a fan of her philosophy, her writing style, or how she conducted her personal life, this is an awesome line. Rand, A. (1996). *The Fountainhead*. Penguin Putnam.

44 In the case of a bio-child or very early adoption. In the case of later adoption, the relationship is still unconditional, even though the child's sense of self may have formed before meeting their parents. (See section below.)

So, what is the basis of unconditional parent → child love? I believe there's only one condition, actually: "Because you're mine." That's it! I'll borrow M. Scott Peck's definition[45] of love: active commitment to another's growth and happiness. "I'm going to be committed and involved in your growth and happiness no matter what you do. Why? Because you're mine." That sounds like parent → child love, right? As a nonparent, it sounds beautiful *and* exhausting. (My friends who are parents have assured me that this is indeed the case.)

Self-Love Should Be Unconditional

Here's what conditional self-love sounds like: "Because I'm great. Because I deserve it. Because I like myself." If you feel these things, great! But they are unstable (because they are conditional) reasons for self-love. The implication is, "If I weren't great, I wouldn't love myself." If you need to have your own back in the long run, you'll need a more solid basis for self-support.

Which is? The exact same reason as above: "Because I'm mine." And why would you be committed to your own growth and happiness? Because you want to grow and be happy! If you want the good for yourself, that's self-love. You might even believe you don't deserve the good. But deserving is different from wanting. (For more, see page 16.) The part of you that just wants the good is the part that loves yourself. I'll quote the ancient Jewish sage Hillel: "If I am only for myself, who will be for me?"[46] You've gotta have your own back. Why? Because you belong to you.

If this is too abstract, here's a very specific example I enjoy using: Why do I brush my teeth regularly? Is it because I'm proud of my teeth? Because I think I *deserve* healthy teeth? Nope, not really. I brush my teeth *because they're mine*. They're going to keep being mine, so I want

---

45 Peck, M. S. (1978). *The Road Less Traveled: A New Psychology of Love, Traditional Values, and Spiritual Growth*. New York, Simon and Schuster.
46 Pirkei Avot 1:14

them to be in good shape for my own sake. That's the long-term goal. In the short term, I brush them because I'm the primary one who has to deal with my own bad breath, and I don't want that for myself either!

Conclusion

Both conditional *and* unconditional love are beautiful things. I'm fairly confident they keep me sane and thriving every day. But! Let's not mistake one for the other. You should conditionally love those who look out for you and whom you look out for as long as the relationship is healthy and nourishing for everyone. You should love unconditionally only those who are ultimately your responsibility—yourself and your children.[47]

---

47 Please do not read this essay as an endorsement of having children. A full life can be lived with or without children. For readers who are wondering about my thoughts on unconditional love for one's pets, it's a fine question. But human ← → pet relationships are outside my expertise as a therapist.

SEE YOURSELF
THROUGH TIME

"Time is a sort of river of passing events, and strong is its current; no sooner is a thing brought to sight than it is swept by, and another takes its place, and this too will be swept away."

— Marcus Aurelius

"I live off a motto that says, 'Yesterday is history, tomorrow is a mystery.' I have goals and agendas. Wherever I'll be tomorrow, that's where I'll be."

— Robert Matthew Van Winkle, a.k.a. Vanilla Ice

You're plagued by memories. You're lost in the moment. You're worried about what happens next and what you'll do. You have this nagging feeling that there was something you were supposed to remember to do.

You're in the forest of time, the trees are the moments, and . . . you're a tree squirrel.

We have a habit of separating humans from animals by claiming only we have an awareness of time, and the tree squirrel proves us wrong.

They need to have a sense of presence—that is, being in touch with where they are in the present moment. It's a literal balancing act—landing on a tree, scampering along strong and delicate branches, and generally maintaining awareness of how their body is or is not stabilized on the tree. The tree squirrel may also treat the tree as a place to rest, nesting among the branches or in a hollow cavity.

They also need to have a sense of the immediate future, which is how they leap from tree to tree. This combines awareness of their position on the current tree with awareness of the surrounding trees. How far away is the next one, and can they jump to it? If they do jump to it, where and how will they land? Will the next one provide better sustenance or safety than the current one? Where will they go after that? These assessments may need to happen in rapid succession, with the squirrel leaping instinctively. Or they may have time to take a more deliberate approach and take stock of the situation before proceeding.

They are also known for preparing for the future, specifically hoarding food before the winter, a.k.a. squirreling away. This requires finding food but not immediately eating it. They need to locate, use, and remember to return to stashes of nuts. They might use a single stash or practice scatter hoarding, which creates smaller stashes that are strategically spread out from each other. Either way, the squirrels need to remember where to return to unearth their stashes. If they fail to remember and retrieve a buried item, it might take root and grow into a tree of its own!

With so much to remember, monitor, and plan for, it's not easy being a creature of time. Thinking of the past, the present, and the future each poses its own challenges, and it's even harder to coordinate your actions across these moments.

If you forget the past, you may repeat your mistakes. If you dwell too much on the past, you'll be unable to thrive in the present. To live well with your past, you'll need to respond gracefully, whenever it comes to mind.

If you forget yourself in the present, you'll lose your grip on immediate reality. If you don't know where and how you're standing, you may slip. If you rush through it and don't watch where you're going, you may fall. In any present moment, you are both *in* that moment and also moving *through* it. To live well with your present, you have to be able to arrive and rest in it while also seeing the next one coming so you don't act impulsively when it arrives.

If you don't envision and plan ahead, you could have a future, but not one of your own making. You can plan for your future in different ways. At some points, you'll care about very large goals (single stashes);

at other times, you'll pursue multiple goals in different areas of your life (scatter hoarding). If you forget aspects of your plan, you might end up in a moment you didn't intend.

The essays in this section will provide reflections on what it means to have a past, present, and future, along with some strategies for living well with each of them. Your life exists in the present moment and is spread across moments through time. If you can keep an eye on yourself in and across time, you will have more control over finding clarity and peace in them.

Take It 1.5 Days at a Time (And Every Day Starts the Night Before)

I started my professional work in addiction counseling, which meant I had a lot of exposure to AA, NA, and the Twelve-Step approach to recovery. Twelve-Step programs are effective for many people on account of the meetings, community, and rituals. But what attracted me the most were the slogans. They are *so good* at slogans! As someone who loves coming up with pithy and powerful phrases, I'm straight-up envious of how many awesome slogans Twelve-Step program members have and use to their benefit.

One classic that's made its way into the general public is "Take it one day at a time." It's wise advice. If someone wants to stay sober for a very long time (possibly forever), that's an overwhelming prospect. But it's unnecessary to think that far ahead. The only questions needed are "How will I stay sober today?" And "What's my plan, just for today?"[48]

In my professional opinion, this approach is useful for any behavior change a person wants to pursue. I might plan out a full schedule to train for a marathon, but I can train only one day at a time. I can focus only on today.

But! Here's my twist, with respect/apologies to those in a Twelve-Step program:

---

48 (1992). *Just for Today: Daily Meditations for Recovering Addicts*. World Service Office.

1. Take it **1.5** days at a time.
2. Every day starts the night before.[49]

So, what exactly is the length of time I'm talking about? It includes:

*   An evening
*   The daytime that follows it
*   The evening following that (which is, of course, the start of the next day as well)

Here's why I'm promoting this variation:

When I'm taking it one day at a time and days are morning-afternoon-evening, I find that the mornings are really hard—even dreadful sometimes. If I'm focused on just one a.m.-to-p.m. day, I don't feel prepared to take on this new day when I wake up. The narrow focus of "just for today" doesn't explicitly include the tasks of logistically and emotionally preparing for the next day.

But if I'm taking it 1.5 days at a time, and if my days start at night, each night can serve as a little preparation for the next morning. I go to sleep a little earlier when I know that very soon, I'll be Morning Matt and that Nighttime Matt has the power to provide or deprive him of the rest he needs. I'm grateful when Nighttime Matt has already prepared my lunch for me. I feel more oriented when I wake up with a to-do list/schedule created the night before. And I'm wayyyy better at getting out of bed when I already know what I've planned on doing next.

Is this too much? Is 1.5 days (and/or starting days at night) burdensome and, therefore, stressful and triggering? If it is, please ignore me. But if you like this, I hope it serves you to take it one day (and just a little more) at a time.

---

49 The second point is not original. I'm borrowing it from my cultural heritage in Judaism, in which all days (including holidays) start in the evening. This is based on Genesis 1:5, "And there was evening and there was morning, one day."

Getting Over It,
Over and Over Again

"I wish I could just get over it."

"I want to put the whole thing behind me and be totally done with it."

You have experiences that still hurt and interactions that left you shaken, sour, bitter, etc.[50] When these experiences come to mind, it's at best annoying and at worst very distressing. Wouldn't it be nice to just get over it? Heck yeah—you'd be grateful to never again rethink and relive that argument, that embarrassment, or that scarring event.

But the past is always inside you, and new situations and stressors can always remind you of whatever you'd rather be done with. With those reminders come an automatic cascade of sensations, emotions, and thoughts. You're having a flashback. The past is once again present, or at least that's what your body-mind[51] thinks.

Even if you're not having flashbacks, when the upsetting experience comes back to mind, you automatically start trying to process it again. There's this thought: *If only I can process this—break it apart, chew on*

---

50 Readers will recognize that traumatic experiences fall under this category of "things that happened that I want to put behind me." For those looking to heal from post-traumatic stress, this chapter may serve as an introduction. But I recommend looking into more in-depth approaches, such as IFS, EMDR, SP, and other acronyms in the world of trauma-focused therapy.

51 Maté, G., & Maté, D. (2022). *The Myth of Normal: Trauma, Illness & Healing in a Toxic Culture.* New York, Avery, an imprint of Penguin Random House.

it, absorb whatever wisdom for life I can take, and excrete the rest[52]*—I'd just be done with it forever, right? Once it's been processed, I've officially gotten over it and can move on. Right?*

Here's the thing: *Getting over it is something you practice, not a one-time event.* If the past is inside, and it can always be stirred up again, getting over it is actually a set of skills for getting resettled as quickly as possible every time you're shaken up by a memory. The better (and faster) you are at getting over it, over and over again, the less the past can plague you, and the less it can eat away at you.

These are the skills involved:

1. Recognizing that the memory has come up

Getting lost in thought can be fun and even productive, or it can be a way to fall into mental pits. You'll need to know which is which—which topics are the stuff of daydreams and which of daymares? It's essential to identify which things from your past torture you when they come to mind. If you're aware of what past things trouble you, you'll have the power to say or think, "Ah, here it is again," when it comes.

2. Allowing the relevant sensations to come and go

By the time you're thinking, *Here it is again*, you're usually already (physically) feeling the effects of having it come to mind. So next, name those sensations, breathe into them, maybe roll your shoulders, stretch or shake out your limbs to reduce tension, and do whatever else you can do to settle yourself physically. Through these physical moves, you've now brought your attention back into the actual present. From this vantage point, you can observe the memory and your reactions without getting sucked into them.

---

52 Processing is an emotional task, but the word itself is borrowed as a metaphor from the realms of eating and manufacturing.

3.   Taking cognitive steps to not get hooked into the habit of rehashing[53] and relieving the past

If you mistake getting over it for a one-time event with the goal of getting some closure once and for all, you'll easily get hooked into the trap of endless reprocessing. Making sense, processing, healing, etc., are very important tasks, but it's better to commit a dedicated time (perhaps in scheduled therapy sessions) to doing that work. If you're just trying to be present in your day, now is not that time. You might even say to yourself, "Hey, I know this is an important thing to process, so how about I devote some time later to it—maybe with my journal or therapist? Right now, I need to focus on the task at hand."

The biggest tool for not getting hooked is self-talk.[54] Here's my example: There's someone who really angered me about two years ago. I'm no longer in touch with them. But they still come to mind for a variety of reasons. When I notice they've come to mind, I say to myself, "Yep, I know. Gah, they suck. They totally do. But is there something I'd like to do about it right now? Is there something that feels worth doing that'll result in a new and satisfying response from them? No new ideas? Well then . . . I guess we better move on for now."

Please note that I'm not saying any of this to shut up that part of me that wants to reprocess. I'm taking it seriously, inviting it to share something new, and, if it doesn't have anything new, inviting it to come back when it's got something new. The sentiment is "You're welcome here, and you're not wrong. But I can't really engage with you unless we're going to do something useful."

Through practice, you learn how to set aside the troubling thought with full awareness and allowance that it will come back again. You're never fully over it, but you can get over it over and over again. If you look at getting over it as a set of skills, you won't feel dread or like a

---

53 There's that food metaphor again . . .
54 Self-talk is a classic recommendation from cognitive therapists. It can be powerful but still limited when it comes to traumatic healing, which is often better served through experiential therapies, as I mentioned in an earlier footnote.

failure when it comes back up. Instead, you'll acknowledge it but also feel too tired to engage with it. The sentiment is "Oh, you again."

You can never erase your past, but you can get better and better at keeping it from taking over your present.

Your Goals (and Your Future) Are Your Weirdest Possessions

It's weird. You have your goals in the present, but your goals are always about your future . . . which doesn't exist yet. You want a particular future to come about, but in the present moment, you have a limited ability to know and shape what that future will be. So, you have your goals as hopes, but you don't have your goals as realities. You have your future as a possibility, but you don't have your future as a reality.

What is going on here?

This bizarre situation is the consequence of (1) having an identity and (2) being subject to time. Your life takes place right this moment and yet also takes place across a period of time. You live *in* the present, but you live *toward* the future. Your life will ultimately span the past, present, and future.

So, what does it mean to have a future and have goals for a future? Because they're such weird possessions, I will compare having future goals to a very specific situation: shopping for shoes during puberty.

Shoe shopping during puberty comes with both biological and social challenges. Biologically, your feet are still growing, which means you're looking for something bigger than your old shoes—big enough to grow into but not so big that you're tripping over yourself now or so big that your feet will never grow into them. Socially, you may feel pressure to buy a certain brand because they're popular or because they look good on your peer role models.

Both size and style play into the functional considerations that come with shoe shopping. Questions abound: If you're trying something outside the norm for you, can you pull off the new look? Are these shoes appropriate for the terrains you want to walk on? Are they comfortable? Are they durable?

Trying on a pair of new shoes brings with it uncertainty and anxiety. They might feel uncomfortable. Is that because they don't fit or because you haven't broken them in yet? They look weird. Is that because they will never look good on you or because you haven't gotten used to your fresh, new style? How are you supposed to interpret your discomfort?

Finally, there's the anxiety of making the purchase. Should you have tried on more shoes? What if nothing is right and you should just go to a new store? Did you find the right ones? What if you regret buying them? If you do regret the purchase and can't return them, do you keep wearing them just to get your money's worth? Or do you take the loss and go shopping again?

The cycle is completed when you start thinking it's time to buy new shoes. Maybe the old ones are wearing thin or you want to try a new style. Maybe they're getting too snug—your feet are growing again. But maybe your feet are actually done growing, and it would be a mistake to trade up yet again. How can you truly know when it's time to move on?

The same kind of challenges arise when you try to imagine your future, choose goals for yourself, and set about accomplishing those goals.

No matter your age, a goal is an expression of what you want to be when you grow up. A goal is a desire to grow. But how much growth is possible, and how long will it take? It's best to develop subgoals, or intermediate goals, so you have a plan for how you'll grow bit by bit into the greatness you seek.[55] If you aim too high all at once, it can be confusing or downright disastrous.

---

55 In psychology, this is called the "zone of proximal development." Vygotsky, L. S. (1978). *Mind in Society: The Development of Higher Psychological Processes*. Massachusetts: Harvard University Press.

We often look to others' goals in trying to figure out our own.[56] This isn't necessarily a bad idea. Certain goals (financial independence, physical health, finding a mate, etc.) are popular for a reason, right? And yet, the future does not have a one-size-fits-all shape. If your vision of the future is borrowed from others, you might end up feeling like you're not living your own life.

When you take on a new goal and start taking steps toward achieving it—and maybe even when you've already achieved it—you might feel . . . not quite right. Why? You're uncomfortable in this new status, and you're wondering whether the discomfort is a sign that you don't actually belong here, a.k.a. you're experiencing imposter syndrome. The thing is, this discomfort is ambiguous. The discomfort of a new shoe can be a sign that it doesn't fit or just a sign that it's not broken in yet. Your imposter syndrome could be a sign that you don't belong or just a sign that it feels weird to be new at something and haven't broken in this new identity or role yet.

There's also the anxiety of choosing your goals at the expense of rejecting other ones. You're experiencing indecision and fear of regret. And if you do find yourself regretting a path in life, now what? It's tempting to fall for the sunk cost fallacy, to stick it out with a flawed goal, just to avoid feeling like your efforts thus far have been a waste.

Finally, there's the question of whether and when it's time to set new goals. If you're feeling restless, it could mean it's time to set your sights further on. Or it could mean you've gotten so used to setting and pursuing goals that it feels weird to simply have arrived.

I'll end with my advice, both for shoe shopping and having future goals:

1. Allow for obsolescence. What worked for you in the past might not keep working for you.

---

56 I first learned this concept of the "mimetic appropriation of desire" from Hans, J. S. (1990). *The Fate of Desire*. State University of New York Press.

2. Don't be paralyzed by fear of failure and waste. It's hard to find what works for you, so expect it to be a process of trial and error. This requires the courage to start all over, sometimes over and over again.

3. Be patient with and curious about your discomfort. Something new may truly not fit. Or maybe it is (and you are) just new. Over time, you'll find out why.

4. Diversify your investments! If you can afford it, it's good to have shoes and goals for different occasions and backup shoes and goals in case of mishaps.

5. It's okay to feel content. A snug life is not such a bad thing; you don't necessarily have to keep growing and transforming. Sometimes, you've found the life size and lifestyle that will work for you forever.

How to Be in the Present— Both of Them!

Presents

It's a saying popularized in the time of the hippies: "Be Here Now."[57] In its original context, it's about focusing your attention (being) on your present place (here) and on your present moment (now). It's a meditative mantra, challenging you to stop living in the past or the future and to simply be in the present. When you are overwhelmed in a situation, you can pause and Be. Here. Now. In the here and now, you are mindful of your body, senses, sensations, and immediate environment. It's a grounding, calming, simplifying mode of being.

And it's incomplete.

There are two different kinds of here and now (henceforth called "presents") you can have in mind and two different modes of awareness— the snapshot present and the storybook present. To thrive in life, you need the commitment and skills to thrive in *both* modes. The snapshot present is the one I've already described, the one touted by mindfulness meditation teachers everywhere.

So—what's the storybook present?

While the snapshot present focuses on a single isolated moment, the storybook present is a reminder that *there's no such thing as an isolated moment*. Every moment takes place in the middle of a larger

---

57 Ram Dass. (1978). *Be Here Now*. Hanuman Foundation.

situation (actually, tons of situations), and each situation takes place in the middle of a larger story (again, tons).

In the snapshot present, you might feel your stomach rumbling. In the storybook present, you're aware of all the details, which give context to this rumbling sensation: When did you last eat, what did you eat, and when will you eat again?

But let's expand that: The rumbling of your stomach might also be understood in the larger contexts of your health, day, year, genetics, access to food and how it's prepared, location in society, location in history, and so on. Your stomach is a plot point (for you, at least) in *many stories.*

I'm highlighting the distinction between the snapshot and the storybook presents in order to make a point about mindfulness. Popular mindfulness practices[58] get you focused only on the snapshot present. Snapshot-present mindfulness is about calming yourself in the immediate present. Part of its destressing power is that you drop the narrative of whatever situation is stressing you out. You are invited to stop thinking about the past and the future, stop thinking about the stories you're in, and take refuge in the immediate present.

But the word *refuge* is telling. For all its virtues (and there are many), snapshot-present mindfulness is also a form of avoidance and side-stepping the bigger challenge: How do you lower your stress *while remaining present in the story itself?* You need skills for being present and calm while actively engaged in the middle of the story—a much harder challenge since the middle of a story is the part with the most confusion and the least resolution.

The Stresses of the Storybook Present

The middle of a story is stressful for three people: the character, the reader, and the writer.

---

58 Kabat-Zinn, J. (1994). *Wherever You Go, There You Are: Mindfulness Meditation in Everyday Life.* Hyperion.

The character is literally[59] in the middle of the story and wondering, *What is going on?* I'll call this *plot ignorance*. The character is disoriented, lacking the full story of how they got there, what's going on with others, and even what's going on inside themselves. And they certainly don't know how it's all going to turn out.

The reader is reading the story and wondering, *What does it all mean?* I'll call this *thematic confusion*. The themes of a story are the ideas—really, the values—running through it. Is this story about loyalty, rebellion, intimacy, independence, security, justice, etc.? Since stories usually have many themes, the reader then has to deal with *thematic conflict*: What's the relationship between these themes? Does one matter more? What's the lesson here?[60]

The writer is writing the story and wondering, *What do I do now?* Let's just call this what it is: *writer's block*. Taking into consideration all the complicated situations and themes, the writer is tasked with deciding on some kind of action that will move forward and maybe even bring resolution to the story.

And here's what makes the middle of life so stressful: *You are all three people.* You are a character, reader, and writer of your story. If it's overwhelming to be one of these people, it's way harder to be all three at once!

Taking Stock

The character, reader, and writer bear the stress of answering their respective questions above. You may freak out when you try to answer those questions frantically. You try to answer frantically because you want resolution as quickly as possible. You want it as quickly as possible because you don't want to feel uncertain, adrift, and indecisive. You're also trying to avoid feeling ashamed about being uncertain, adrift, and indecisive.

---

59 Or rather, literarily.
60 Sincere apologies to any readers having flashbacks to English class.

I want to offer the process of taking stock as a set of skills and practices for addressing storybook questions. Notice my language—I said "addressing," not "answering," questions. In taking stock, you may or may not find definitive answers. But I can promise that you will be better able to reflect on your situation (instead of avoiding it) without freaking out.

What are the skills of taking stock?

1. Gathering up (observing, analyzing, brainstorming, daydreaming) details about the situation
2. Playing around with ways of putting these details together
3. Generating many answers (rather than The Answer) to your question

This may sound abstract, so let's put it this way instead: Brainstorm and make a bunch of lists.

Here's what that looks like for the character, reader, and writer:

The **character** wants to know what's going on. Well, list the details! What are the details here—the people, places, things, feelings, attitudes, actions, challenges, goals, etc.? What are the moving parts? What appears to be causing what?

Now that you have brainstormed a giant list of details, generate more and more versions of the story by arranging and rearranging the details. What's your perspective? What are the other characters' perspectives? What would a total outsider see?

By holding many versions of the story, it's harder to get lost in a single, dominating one. The character can avoid freaking out by looking at their situation in the spirit of exploration, curiosity, and the willingness to learn and be corrected. More details shed more light; different angles lead to different answers.

The **reader** wants to know what matters in the story and what motivates the characters. Well, list the themes and values! If the story is confusing because there are many values at stake, identify as many values as possible, reflect on why you value them, and determine how the conflict of these values makes it hard for you to feel only one way about what's going on.

Making such a list should bring you some self-compassion. Of course you're confused—it's confusing! Anyone seeing their situation as simple is likely missing something. Anyone blaming themselves for being complicated is failing to honor the fact that being a person is complicated.

The reader of life can avoid freaking out by looking at their situation in the spirit of inclusive love. All of these values matter to you. Your confusion and conflict are authentic, so don't hate yourself for feeling confused and conflicted. You don't yet have to figure out what to do next; just honor the fact that the struggle is real. Accompanied by self-compassion instead of shame, your process of sorting through what it all means will still be complicated, but at least it's no longer humiliating.

The **writer** wants to know what to do next. Well, list the options! Brainstorm options using what I call the fictional approach: List options regardless of whether they will be realistic, effective, or even moral. The goal isn't to come up with the best options but just to get the imagination flowing. The more options listed, the more you can reflect on what you want, what's realistic, and what's good.

Admittedly, the writer still has the hardest task of the three. The writer is challenged not simply to interpret life but ultimately to take concrete action. You experience the storybook present as a crossroads, a precipice, a one-way-no-return door into the future. That's heavy! What if the decision goes poorly?

Facing the possibility of a poor outcome, the writer can keep making lists—next steps, contingency plans, and worst-case-scenario plans. From the perspective of the storybook present, you are always in the middle of a situation, which means you can always make new lists of what might come next. That's the good and bad news: There's always more future to consider.

Zooming Out

All these practices for taking stock will lead to you having a bunch of lists—of details, perspectives, values, and possibilities in your story. But looking at a pile of lists can still be overwhelming! How exactly does storybook-present mindfulness reduce your chances of freaking out?

Let's contrast it again with snapshot-present mindfulness. Snapshot-present mindfulness brings calm by guiding you to look away from your stories and into your body. The situation is a mess, so you feel like a mess. Meditation enables you to step away from the situation to calm your inner turmoil. The issue, as I noted above, is that meditation leaves the mess of the situation unaddressed. You meditate, but the mess awaits your return.

Storybook-present mindfulness calms you by keeping your focus on the story, *except now you're standing above it.* It's the difference between being lost in a forest and being lost while looking at a map of the forest. With a map, with a bunch of lists, you can treat your situation like a story to ponder. You gain the breathing room afforded to the reader and writer (and not to the character).

If you think about the phrase "moving parts," it becomes clear why list-making is so essential. In a situation with a lot of moving parts, it's hard to keep track of everything and even harder to imagine where to put it all. By writing out the various moving parts (detail, themes, possibilities) into points on a list, you make it far easier (literally by cutting and pasting) to move them around. You can try out one way of organizing it all, then jumble them back up and try out a different way. To use a related metaphor, before taking action (intense!), you can play with action figures (far more relaxing).

In talking about lists and zooming out, let's review the advantages of using storybook-present mindfulness:

- It's better to be mindful than lost in a situation because, by stepping slightly outside the situation, you have more room to be intentional in your thinking, feeling, and acting.[61]

---

61 Of course, being lost can be great in certain situations, such as "losing yourself to dance." Daft Punk. (2013). "Lose Yourself to Dance" [Song]. On *Random Access Memories.* Columbia Records.

- Storybook-present mindfulness is better than snapshot-present mindfulness because, even though you've stepped *out* of the situation, you're still looking *toward* it. While snapshot-present mindfulness can provide a much-needed break *away* from the situation altogether, you'll still need a way to be calm *while* thinking about the situation—which is what storybook-present mindfulness provides.
- The list-making of storybook-present mindfulness is, while still a kind of mental work, more relaxing than trying to figure it all out in real time. Think of the commerce metaphor in play here—taking stock (of inventory in the store's quiet back room with a clipboard and some shelves) is way less chaotic than the hustle and bustle of the store floor.

Conclusion

You can avoid freaking out by taking an interest in all the details, nuances, and possibilities in your story, then taking some prep time to consider them without any immediate need to solve and take action. Traditional snapshot-present mindfulness serves you when you need a break from trying to sort it all out. Storybook-present mindfulness serves you when you need to sort it all out without freaking out.

Before trying to swim across the ocean (daunting!), you should splash around in it for a while (playful!). Yes, figuring it all out is important and even urgent. But those feelings of pressure and urgency are overwhelming and stressful. Achieving some level of calm serves you better in the task. So, before racing to conclusions, just take stock.

The last skill I need to mention is discernment, a.k.a. the wisdom to know the difference. You'll need some sense of when to engage with the snapshot present and when to engage with the storybook present. Knowing when to engage with the snapshot present is easy. If you're feeling physically and emotionally overwhelmed and overheated by the effort to figure it all out, it's time for a snapshot-present mindfulness break.

But! It's only a mindfulness *break* (rather than a full-on *escape*) if you then return to engaging with the story, so . . . how do you know when it's time to switch back to the story? You're ready once snapshot-present mindfulness has calmed down your body. Feeling a bit more settled and grounded, you're now ready to be curious and open. You've slowed your whole system down and can now feel emotionally available to take on the uncertainty and confusion involved in trying to make sense of the story. And if that storybook-present mindfulness gets overwhelming (even standing aside from the mess, it can feel a lot just to look at it), it's time to switch back again.

Life is a lot to be mindful of; you'll need a lot of ways to be mindful.

HEALTHY RELATIONSHIPS REQUIRE SHARING POWER AND REALITY

"The dialogue between you and I is the essence of life."

— Martin Buber

"I knew when I met you an adventure was going to happen."

— Winnie the Pooh, A. A. Milne)

You're angry at your friend. Angry and sad. And confused. If you're friends, how does this keep happening? It feels like you each have to compete for attention and care. Sometimes, it feels like you're each there only for your own benefit, not the other's. Sometimes, you feel pushed away; other times, you're the one doing the pushing. There's no understanding. There's no cooperation.

You're in the forest of relationships, and you are trees, standing together and yet apart.

It's confusing that trees are both individual and communal organisms. Each one has its own life and death, even as that life and that death are shaped almost entirely by the environment. The individual tree is nourished and protected by the trees around it. And it can very often be in competition for resources with those same trees. Roots can compete for access to water and soil nutrients. Canopies compete for sunlight. They can injure each other through friction and suffocate each other through closeness. But also, some trees, subject to friction, will grow into one another!

To live well in the forest, a tree needs to be connected to its environment. Recent popular scientific interest in trees has focused on mycorrhizal networks—filaments of fungi intertwined with the tips of tree roots—through which trees appear to share resources and information with one another.

Trees must also be protected from their environment. Some trees survive fires by having thick bark and deep roots. In hot areas, some trees can survive drought by controlling moisture lost through their leaves. In colder regions, most trees have flexible branches that can shed the heavy load of accumulating snow. To live well together, they need to stay connected and separate.

It's confusing that humans are individual and communal. You are the only one living your life, and yet most humans live their individual lives around other humans doing that same thing. You can be nourished, protected, deprived, and threatened by other people—sometimes even by the same people! When resources are limited, tensions run high. You develop intimacy through close contact with others. You can also develop contempt.

How can we be together in healthy ways? Certainly, we can cooperate to survive and thrive by sharing information and resources. And yet, taking care of ourselves as individuals is just as important. Pulling back for personal space can be essential to the sustainability of a close relationship. We can work to be less sensitive and less easily injured by others by having thicker skin, a more established sense of self, the flexibility to let things go, and the ability to hold back from losing our being to someone else. Good boundaries make good relationships.

There's an important difference, though, between forest relationships and human relationships. We have the capacity to *work at it*. Trees and other plants follow set patterns, cooperating and competing in ways that have evolved slowly over time and don't change within the course of a single tree's lifetime. As humans, we need to and can do better than that. To maintain healthy interpersonal and communal relationships, we have to respond much quicker to conflicts. We need ways to reflect and change ourselves and ways to reflect along with the other and change the relationship.

The essays in this section address many of the ways interpersonal relationships become strained and provide insights and advice for working it out together.

Should You Be Selfish or Selfless? Neither— It's Time to Self-Inhabit

Selfish and *selfless* are opposites. Yet neither is a useful word for capturing the balancing act that is balancing self-care and care of others. As a therapist, I'm finding the selfish/selfless binary *very annoying*. Here's why: Clients keep getting caught up in it, asking things like "I feel bad about being selfish, but aren't I allowed to be selfish sometimes?" and "I'm such a people pleaser, but it's worse to be selfish, right?" Unsure how to balance selfish vs. selfless, people are likely to swing back and forth between the two, impulsively overcorrecting their attitudes and actions and, in the process, hurting themselves and others.

There's a historical tradition of struggling with this binary, as famously expressed by Ayn Rand. She typifies Christian morality as dangerous and abusive by demanding that we be selfless, as expressed in verses like "No one should seek their own good, but the good of others."[62] Criticizing the selfless approach to life, she champions its opposite in books like *The Virtue of Selfishness*. While Rand is known for a kind of radical selfishness that defies any concern for others, she also hints at how selfishness can serve as a secure base in our caring relationships: "To say 'I love you' one must first know how to say the 'I.'"[63] For her, selfishness may be a fundamental virtue, but it is one that can also support our relational endeavors.[64]

---

62 2 Corinthians 10:24.
63 Rand, Ayn. *The Fountainhead*. Penguin Putnam, 1996.
64 "Relational endeavors" may be an odd phrasing choice, but it felt more fitting than to imagine Ayn Rand believing in such a thing as "relational needs."

In the Jewish tradition, Rabbi Hillel the Elder is known for his saying: "If I am not for myself, who will be for me? If I am only for myself, what am I?"[65] He is also caught in the tension between being for self and being for others. Here again, it is clear that the words *selfish* and *selfless* do not set us up for success when it comes to thinking straight about taking care of ourselves and others.

And so I present to you my current best offer for solving this dilemma with the following term: *Self-inhabiting*, to be used as a modifier ("I'm working on living a more self-inhabiting lifestyle") or a verb ("I need to remember to self-inhabit instead of only being selfish or selfless").

It's a metaphor. To self-inhabit means you are at home in your self. By "self," I mean body, mind, time, energy, needs, wants, goals, relationships, values, beliefs, doubts, likes, dislikes, and all those things that are yours, including your actual home.

This—all of this—is your home. Therefore, it's your job to tend to it. You live here. You know its ins and outs. You know (and continue to learn over time) its strengths and weaknesses, and it falls on you to address whatever it is that needs addressing. It's a sacred trust. You belong to you; you are yours. Your needs and desires are yours to be managed as needed and to sometimes be prioritized over those of others. You might spend all your time (literally or figuratively) cleaning others' homes. But at the end of the day, you'd still have to return to live in your own neglected space.

But here's where the metaphor can be cleverly extended: If you're self-inhabiting, it means you have the ability to host guests![66] But it will feel better to host guests when you have a chance to clean up first. You can invite someone into your home only if it's somewhere you already feel at home. When your space feels good to live in, it feels good to invite others into it. Welcoming others into your space is a blessing—a bit of grace. If you think of your personal space as something you carry

---

65 Pirke Avot 1:14.
66 With thanks for Sri Sri Ravi Shankar's "The Art of Living Class" for this central insight/metaphor.

around with you, you always have this opportunity to provide a warm welcome to being with you. But! It's still *your* home to do with as *you* wish. Sometimes, what you might need is to keep to yourself and spend some time not letting others in.

What I love about the host/guest metaphor is that the two roles have boundaries. You should care for your guests—maybe even at some expense to yourself, but not to the point of self-neglect or self-harm. Here's the important fact about guests—*they are not the host.* A bad guest can and should be asked to leave, even kicked out if needed. As a host, you have the right to invite someone to visit as well as to leave. My rabbi in college would end Sabbath dinners by saying, "Thanks for coming and thanks for going."[67] Now that's some good hosting! The guest has the right to be welcomed warmly and graciously; they do not have the right to hijack your residence. "But they would be so disappointed if I pushed them out!" is unfortunately not a blanket justification for letting them push you around.

Take the example of hosting a game night. A good host considers what games their guests already enjoy . . . but these should also be games the host enjoys, right? What's the point in having people over to play a game you don't even like? At the same time, it's good for both host and guests to be open to each other. It can be a blessing for the host, comfortable in their own space, to introduce a new game they think the guests will like. Similarly, it's a blessing for the guests to bring an offering, such as a new game that could be a fun new addition to the household. If it's not too uncomfortable for either host or guests, they can even take turns trying each other's games. Unfortunately, if there are no mutually enjoyable games or, even worse, there are only games that are dangerous to one or the other, the party should end. The comfort of all involved parties is paramount to any party, literal or metaphorical.

Self-inhabiting allows for hosting, and hosting is a fine balance between taking care of guests and oneself. If you're not sure what to do

---

67 Rabbi Yonah Blum, personal communication, 2001-2005.

with yourself in a relationship, don't ask, "Well, should I be selfish or selfless?" Instead, ask, "What can I do to take care of my space *and* my guest right now?" Sometimes, that means taking care of only one of you, at least for a while. "It's been good having you over. Now I need some time to settle into my self."

Everything People
Do Makes Sense
(Even the Nonsense)

"Why would they do that?"
"That made *no* sense."
"They did that for *no* reason."

When someone does something that makes no sense to you, it will look like nonsense. But with enough background information, *everything* people do makes sense.

This is not to say that everything we do is justified or even practical. There are such things as terrible and stupid actions, but I'm saying that even misbehavior[68] has internal logic.

What do I mean by internal logic? Another way to express this would be to take the saying "Everything happens for a reason" and change it to "Everything happens due to causes."

Asserting that everything happens for a reason is an expression of absolute optimism and meaningfulness. The message is "Don't be angry/scared/sad—everything happens for a reason!" It implies that everything that happens is justified. This incessantly positive attitude is problematic because it takes away your ability to criticize anything or anyone.[69]

---

68 At the risk of understating the severity of various terrible and stupid actions, I'll be calling it all "misbehavior" from this point on.

69 This "for a reason" sentiment is often backed up by faith in an all-knowing, all-powerful, and all-good God. If this theology brings you comfort, go for it. Just be aware that it might not be as comforting to other people.

On the other hand, asserting that everything happens due to causes inspires curiosity about those causes. It motivates you to piece together how this misbehavior made sense at the time, even if it was the wrong thing to do. By looking into the myriad causes behind anyone's actions, you start to treat everyone as full human beings with inner lives as complex as your own. It's not just you. Everyone out here is trying to figure out what's going on and what to do about it.

My favorite way to make this point is by referring to my time working with recovering addicts. To outsiders, and often to the addicts themselves, their drug use doesn't make any sense. The damning thought is always something like *If they really cared [about themselves, their health, their future, their family, etc.], they wouldn't do their drug... so obviously, they don't care. If they do care, their use doesn't make any sense.* The addict may think, *I know this isn't good for me, so why do I keep doing it? I'm not making any sense!*

This condemnation is oblivious to the internal logic of addiction.[70] Here's one way addiction can make sense: Many addicts take their drug to dull the emotional pain of trauma and stave off the emotional and physical pain of withdrawal (if they were to stop taking their drug). Because the drug serves a crucial emotional need, the choice becomes harder. In any given moment, they can:

1. Take the drug.

    (a) Pro: Gain short-term relief from the emotional pain of trauma and withdrawal.
    (b) Con: Cause and risk further harm from drug use.

2. Abstain from the drug.

    (c) Pro: Begin recovery, begin to restore bodily health and safety, and open the possibility of other ways to heal from trauma.

70 Khantzian, E. J., & Albanese, M. J. (2008). *Understanding Addiction as Self Medication: Finding Hope Behind the Pain.* Rowman & Littlefield.

(d) Con: Experience the pain of emotional trauma without any
buffer or defense.

This is not a simple choice! The pain of the drug feels more manageable
than the pain of traumatic memory. The drug may kill them someday,
but being flooded by traumatic symptoms can make someone feel like
they're going to die—so it's not a simple choice.

This doesn't mean they *should* keep choosing their drug. It just
means that it makes sense that someone *would* keep choosing their drug.
There are a variety of forces pushing and pulling the addict in various
directions, so their misbehavior makes sense. Addictive behavior has
an internal logic to it.

Why is it important that we recognize and honor the internal logic
of misbehavior? Because you can't change your patterns unless you first
understand how they make sense. The addict who thinks, *It's simple.
Drugs are bad, and sobriety is good. Therefore, I'll just stay sober*, is very
likely going to relapse.[71] The addict who recognizes the internal logic
of addiction will think instead, *Sobriety is the healthier option, but my
drug use must be serving my needs in some way. I won't be able to stay
sober unless I learn how to get those needs met*. They are better prepared
to make sense of sobriety once they've made sense of their drug use.

The phrase *internal logic* may be overly intellectual, so let's talk
about its emotional equivalent: *compassion*. If you appreciate (or at least
assume) the internal logic of people's actions, you can feel compassion.
You can do this even while disagreeing. The condescending line "Bless
their heart" actually captures this sentiment pretty well. From your
vantage point, the other person is wrong, but you can allow for the
integrity of their position:

- "I don't want to feel this way, but it makes sense that I feel this way."
- "I'm angry at you for acting this way, but I understand where that
  action came from."

---

71 This was often the case in treatment—whoever showed up most confident was also most
likely to relapse.

That's right—you can feel compassionate *and* angry at the same time. You can make sense of someone's actions even while condemning them.

My most intense experience of this came to me in Charlottesville on August 12, 2017. I was there serving as mental health first aid[72] for protesters against the Unite the Right rally. I've lived a rather sheltered life, so this was my first time being face-to-face with people who very clearly and violently opposed my beliefs and values. I saw them as angry, armored, and armed. And, weirdly, my first thought was, *Wow, those people look scared. Why would someone show up somewhere dressed like that if they weren't scared?* In that moment, I had this deep understanding that, as terrible and mistaken as I believed they were, these people made sense to themselves. I felt compassion for them as I imagined how scared they must be.

And again, again, again, none of my compassion made me hate them or oppose them less. For those scared individuals who are looking to hurt others, I still want them disarmed or shown the error of their beliefs and ways. I would like to fix their internal logic, but first, I have to understand it.

For less intense examples than addiction and white supremacist terrorism, you can think about mundane interactions you have with family, friends, and coworkers. Somebody does something wrong, and you think or ask, "Why would you do that?" It would be a good question . . . if only you were asking it genuinely instead of rhetorically! If you were truly curious about why they did that, you might learn more about what they were thinking. Then you'd have a better chance of having your critical feedback being both informed and appreciated.

A note about phrasing. Genuinely asking, "Why would you do that?" can still come off as an attack rather than a question. It might be better to say something like "What were you going for here?" or "What was your process here?" With questions like this, you're (hopefully)

---

72 Full disclosure: Crisis work has never been a skill of mine, so it would be truer to say I was supporting the people providing the mental health first aid rather than actually administering it myself.

expressing that you haven't made sense of their actions but aren't declaring that their actions made no objective sense. The goal is to have the other feel invited to *explain* themselves rather than pressured to *justify* themselves.

This same insight—about making sense and explaining rather than justifying—works equally well when you're the one being criticized. Imagine you're the one who misbehaved and you know it was misbehavior (e.g., you know you should've done better). If you're confronted, especially if you're confronted in an uncompassionate way, you'll want to explain and show that what you did made sense, even if it was wrong. The problem is that your attempt to explain what you did may be seen as an attempt to justify it! But you can avoid this issue by clarifying your intentions. You can say, "Here's why I did it . . . but that's no excuse," or, "I'm not trying to justify what I did, but I want to explain what was going on for me when I did it." By saying it this way, you're asking for compassion without asking to be let off the hook.

If someone's (or even your own) thoughts and actions don't make sense to you, it might be important to critique and change those thoughts and actions. But you can't effectively criticize or change anything until you've made sense of it.

Why We Yell and How
to Shut Each Other Up
(Maturely)

I like to think of myself as a pretty laid-back person, but . . . well, I can also be a hothead. Sometimes, in arguments, I just get so frustrated. I hate it when I feel like the other person isn't really hearing me. I get loud, and I repeat myself. When I get loud, that usually leads the other person to get loud as well. Then, of course, I hate being yelled at, so when I'm yelled at, I just end up yelling back. Things escalate—we both get loud and repetitive, and we go in circles. We get mad, we get nowhere, we give up on discussing it, and we eventually give up on each other. Why is this happening, and else what can I do?

Here's an analogy I've found helpful for myself:

When else do I get loud and repetitive . . . but *not* angry? When the other person literally has a hard time hearing me. They might be hard of hearing, or maybe we are hanging out at a concert or a crowded, poorly lit bar. Right? I say something, and they say, "What?" So I say it again but louder. If they say, "What?" again, I get even louder. I'm getting loud and repetitive. If it goes on for long enough, I say, "Eh, forget it." I give up on communicating, at least in this environment. Of course, there's no anger involved here, at least not at the other person.

It's pretty much the same thing in an argument. If I feel you didn't hear (understand or appreciate) what I said, I'm gonna repeat myself and get loud. Maybe *this time* I'll get through to you! Meanwhile, since

I'm just repeating myself and getting loud, that means you probably don't feel like you're getting through to me. So you also get loud and repetitive—and there's the vicious cycle.

So how do we (maturely) silence each other? By proving that we understand both what the other is saying and why they are saying it. If I feel you get my point (even if you still disagree with it), I won't feel the need to repeat it. And when you feel heard, you are more likely to return that favor to me. We each listen, and we each feel understood. Once we both understand each other, we're able to move on to further points and are no longer going in circles.

Sounds nice, right? But there are (at least) three challenges to overcome:

1. At least one person has to remember this practice (of listening and demonstrating understanding).

Like I said, I can be a hothead. I think a major factor here is that I get hyper-focused on my own need for recognition from the other and feel like that's all that matters now. I get righteously indignant. I might even move from feeling unheard to feeling disrespected, and the other person is now an enemy to be conquered. Now, *that's* some escalation! How do I emotionally break out of it?

Here's what I've figured out so far: I've had to become much more sensitive to my own emotional escalation, noticing what's happening in my head, body, and behavior. When I notice myself escalating, I remember how much I've burned myself out doing this. Instead of getting worked up, I start getting tired. I remember how much being a hothead tires me out and gets me nowhere. (For more on this point, see the next essay.) And then I switch gears.

2. Both people have to be committed to this practice.

When I'm the only one taking the time, effort, and care to show understanding to the other, I'll feel proud of myself! I'm being the bigger person. But . . . I'll also feel like a sucker—I acted like an adult, but they're still acting like a child! They get to feel heard and validated, but they can't or won't do the same for me! What the heck? In situations like this, I may feel proud of myself, but I'm still more likely to avoid this person (or, at least, certain topics with this person) in the future.

Alternatively, I might try to encourage the other person to join me in this practice. I could say: "I'm working to change how I handle myself in difficult conversations by first making sure I understand your point before I make my own point. I think if I do this, you'll feel more understood and not as angry. What do you think of that? What if you did that too?" (For more on this kind of process comment, see page 213.)

3. Someone has to be the first one to demonstrate understanding of the other's message instead of getting their own message across first.

If I've escalated and you've escalated, what we've got is a standoff—a power struggle. If I back down, I'll seem weak, and they'll win! Heck no. I came here to win! *They* should be the one who backs down!

Sigh. If we're in a relationship together and hope to continue to be in a relationship after this argument, if one person wins, nobody wins. The loser will feel conquered, bad about themselves, or simply resentful. You won the battle, but the war continues. We start keeping score. I backed down the last two times, so now it's your turn to back down. Anger and competition breed further anger and competition.

I've had two different romantic partners who were major role models for initiating this "first demonstrate understanding" approach. One of them was consistently the first to de-escalate, take a step back, and make me feel heard. And every time they did it, I would have these emotional reactions:

1. Gratitude
2. The desire to return the gift
3. Embarrassment that I didn't do it first.

Oh man, they were the bigger person again. Why am I so stubborn? But their maturity would remind me to be mature, and I tried to pick up the slack and give them the gift of being heard first.

The other would de-escalate in a really inspirational way: They would go from being in the fight and angry to being sad that we were fighting at all. Instead of being oriented toward winning or losing the fight, they would reorient back to the relationship and the desire to be on the same team, even if we were disagreeing about something.

It's beautiful, right? This lesson has served me as an additional reminder to practice good listening. It's not just that I hate the feeling of emotional escalation but also that I hate the feeling of having a troubled connection with someone else.

Conclusion

Our need for connection is at the heart of all this striving with others. You feel connected when you feel understood and that you make sense because someone else gets it. And that's the trouble—it's the other person who has the power to give you that feeling or not. They hold that power, and if they fail to provide it, you can resent them for it. You get louder, trying to break through and desperate not to be alone in your reality. But getting loud and aggressive backfires, and now you're each pulling even further away from the other.

You can break the cycle only by first focusing on how you can offer understanding rather than receiving it. You can be inspired to offer understanding by recognizing that the other is driven by that same need for connection. You have that in common. When you both reorient toward that need, you don't want to fight and don't care about winning. You take a step back from all the yelling and start listening instead.

About to Talk with Someone Difficult? Bring These Two Goals

Note: This chapter was largely inspired by the fantastic book Adult Children of Emotionally Immature Parents.[73]

Difficult discussions are even harder when you're having them with a difficult person. Who counts as a difficult person? That may vary by culture and personal preference, so I'll just describe it from my perspective. During a difficult conversation, a difficult person:

- Interrupts
- Gets louder and louder
- Keeps repeating the same talking points
- Attacks, calls names, and displays other aggressive behaviors
- Does not attempt to gain understanding or compassion for my side of things

As you can imagine, it's very difficult to get your point across to a difficult person—and getting your point across (or stated more virtuously, "achieving mutual understanding") is usually the number-one goal in a difficult conversation.

When it feels impossible to fulfill goal number one, you can find yourself getting more agitated and aggressive. You become difficult as well. Well, I know I do. Pardon the obscenity, but I often find that I

---

73 Gibson, P., & Gavin, M. (2016). *Adult Children of Emotionally Immature Parents.* Unabridged. [United States], Tantor Media, Inc.

will lose my s**t (henceforth called "losing it") in such conversations. I get loud and maybe a little aggressive, and I'm no longer interested in listening to someone who isn't listening to me. (For more, see "Why We Yell and How to Shut Each Other Up (Maturely)" on page 142.) But then I'll feel regretful after losing it because of how I treated the other person and because I like to see myself as having more self-control than that.

So, how do you change such behavior? *By having a secondary goal— and not losing it!* The sentiment here is "If I can't get through to them, at least I'll be able to take some pride in how I handled myself." Easier said than done. In the remainder of this essay, I want to develop three key principles for achieving this second goal.

1. Set intentions and remain mindful.

If you know who or what triggers your anger, you can see it coming. Seeing the frustration that lies in dealing with this person, you can set the intention to value keeping calm over getting your point across.

But sometimes, you don't see it coming. This is why it's important to learn to recognize your own agitation based on physical cues (muscle tension, increased heart rate, feeling hot, etc.) or behavioral cues (making a fist, shaking your head, fidgeting, etc.). If you can notice these cues, you'll have a higher chance of switching to your secondary goal.

Even if you don't notice your anger before it turns into impulsivity— good news! Mindfulness is helpful no matter when it enters your mind. "Oh, wow, I'm getting loud over here. I'd really rather not do it further. It makes sense that I'm frustrated, but I'm not interested in getting so worked up over it."

2. Speak up for your own sake, not theirs.

If they're utterly resistant to understanding you, why bother speaking up at all? Because it can be a relief to speak your truth, say it aloud instead of keeping it in, and affirm yourself even while giving up on your desire for their validation. Being plainly (rather than aggressively) assertive might bring you some satisfaction later. "At least I said it."

3. Let them have the last word but without conceding.

Giving up on getting them to get it may give them the impression that they won. For me, not losing it requires that at some point, I no longer engage in the conversation. And that likely means they will have the last word. This is a hard thing to swallow. Yet it's sometimes unavoidable. But you can still indicate that you're not conceding. Assertively, you might say, "I can see we're not getting anywhere, so I don't think we should keep discussing this." Or, if you like some good ol' passive aggression, you can say, "Look, I don't mind if you're not convinced."[74] Then they make their point again, and you say, "Okay," and politely take your leave.

Conclusion

It's very frustrating when your efforts to be understood and validated get nowhere. Anger is an appropriate, if unhelpful, response. (For more, see "Trusting the Anger but Not the Impulse" on page 93.) You want greater power over the other and over the situation, and anger is an expression of that desire for power. Unfortunately, when you lose it, you've actually lost power over your own energy and impulsivity. That's why goal number two (not losing it) is so important. If you can't have power over them, at least you can have power over yourself.

Lastly, a note on terms: I've intentionally used the phrase "not losing your s**t" rather than what may be the more obvious phrase, "Staying calm." I'm avoiding the phrase "Staying calm" because that can refer both to peaceful behavior and inner peace. In a frustrating situation, inner peace may be unrealistic and unnecessary for what I'm promoting. Anger is an important emotion, and it's fine to be mad. I'm just advocating for an approach that avoids the waste of energy and the regret of losing it.

---

74 I wouldn't recommend using this line in an antagonistic situation, but it is a fun way to troll friends during a friendly argument.

How to Confront Your Loved Ones Lovingly

Honesty may be the best policy. But as a virtue, it should never stand alone. When else does someone feel the need to say, "I'm just being honest," other than in a tense exchange? Or that other gem: "I'm not being rude or blunt—I'm being honest." Both statements are very telling. The "just honest" person admits that they are *only* honest, meaning honest, but nothing else—not any other loving trait, such as gentleness, compassion, or even tact. The "I'm not rude, I'm honest" person mistakenly believes that an honest statement cannot, at the same time, be rude.

What's my critique of these folks? Briefly, they may be right, but they're not relational. Or, as Jeffrey Lebowski would (crudely) put it, "You're not wrong . . . you're just an asshole!"[75]

You might be asking, "But what if the truth I need to share is indeed a harsh truth? What if I love someone, and my loved one is in need of a rude awakening? Is it okay to be harsh and rude then?"

I'm not trying to be the authority on when something is okay. My issue isn't that rudeness is wrong but that it gets in the way of the other person being open to your honesty. An honest point, made rudely, is more likely to be rejected without full consideration. An honest point, presented lovingly, goes further. Here is a silly example: "You stink—go take a shower!" may be honest, but it's less effective than something like "I enjoy being around you, and a shower would only improve the experience."

I'm drawing here from the delicate balance required from me as a therapist. Strangers come to me for help, and they often need both

75 Coen, J., & Coen, E. (1998). *The Big Lebowski*. Gramercy Pictures (I).

support *and* challenge. A therapist who only supports is a yes-man, denying the client the opportunity to change and grow. A therapist who only challenges . . . well, it gets annoying and tiring to be challenged all the time, doesn't it? When you have a friend who persistently challenges you, are they ever your favorite one?

As a cognitive therapist, I aim to critique people in such a way that they feel inspired to give me a heartfelt "Thank you!" as they leave. Why specifically cognitive therapy? Because much of my work involves exposing people's irrational thought patterns, and I dare you to find a way to call someone irrational and have them thank you for it.

And yet, to be effective, criticizing must be done lovingly. So, how do you do it?

1. Join them.

In therapist training, expressions of support and empathy are known as joining the client. Without joining your loved one, they can feel misunderstood and isolated. This is fair. If you fail to grasp the gravity and stuckness of their experience, your suggestions and strategies will reflect your lack of understanding. If you invalidate their interpretations and emotions, they will feel all alone and not open to any outside suggestions and strategies.

What does joining sound like? Aim for some variation on "You make sense, and your feelings make sense." If you truly understand their perspective and how they arrived at it, this will be easy to do, even if you think they are 100 percent wrong. If you disagree with them, you can still authentically say, "I can see why this would be hard," which is a way of validating without actually agreeing.

A note on this last phrase, "I can see why this would be hard." Say it only if you actually *can* understand! And if you can't understand them, check yourself before challenging them further. The effectiveness of joining isn't simply a matter of tact, as if making the other feel joined means your feedback will be useful to them. No—your feedback will be unhelpful (or even harmful) if it comes from you thinking the other person doesn't make sense. (For more, see "Everything People Do Makes Sense (Even the Nonsense)" on page 137.)

2.   Get consent to critique.

You'll know they feel joined when they say something like "Yes, that's it, exactly. Thank you." Now they can be open to your challenge! But don't leap in with the challenge. Get consent first with something like one of the following:

- "I'd like to push back a bit though. Is that okay?"
- "Do you mind if I weigh in?"
- "I want to add a couple of additional thoughts. Are you open to that?"

A critical note about consent: You have to wait to see if they actually give it! There's nothing virtuous about asking for consent and then plowing ahead without receiving a positive answer. Similarly, if they reject your offer, you have to receive that rejection graciously: "Okay, thanks for saying what you need." If you sulk or shut down after your offer is rejected, you're punishing them for saying no.[76]

3.   Frame your critique as adding to their perspective, not replacing it.

Broadly, this will be some variation on "What you're saying makes sense. And I want to bring in an additional thought. I hope my thought makes sense and can add to your understanding or approach to the situation." When you use this formula, they won't feel like you are shooting down what they are saying. You are saying, "Yes and" to it.[77]

---

76 Whether you intend or not.
77 Besser, M., Roberts, I., and Walsh, M. (2013). *The Upright Citizens Bridge Comedy Improvisation Manual.* Comedy Council of Nicea. For more on the applicability of improv techniques for personal problem-solving, see "How to Be Good at Being Clueless" on page 67.

Most often, I find that my feedback is welcome and productive when I express both my understanding and my critique in terms of goals. Here's an example from my days as the drug and alcohol educator on a college campus: "It sounds like you wanted to have a good time, and who doesn't? And yet you partied in a way that ended with you in the ER. What if we strategize together about how to party safely so you have a good time *and* wake up safely in your own bed?" The students didn't feel judged for their drinking. They felt joined in their desire to party, now with added considerations about how to do so in a more intentional way.

Conclusion

Well, what do you think? Is this useful? Does it add up? If you have any critiques, let me know: (1) What works in this and[78] (3) What you'd add or change to make it work even better. If I feel you understand what I'm saying and appreciate what I'm attempting to do, I'll be open and interested in critical feedback. You can be honest without being rude.

---

78 I skipped #2, "Get consent to critique." You won't need to do that step because I'm giving consent right now.

It's Not Just You:
Socializing Is Weird

Social anxiety is real, but not all discomfort around people is social anxiety. According to the DSM-5,[79] an essential element of social anxiety is fear of being judged by others. But—please understand—socializing can be *super awkward* whether or not it's anyone's fault. Stop (always) blaming yourself for awkward social situations!

Now, it could be your fault, and that's why examining and criticizing yourself can be a virtue . . . unless it's self-criticism run rampant that's *always* focusing blame *entirely* on you. Instead, let's take a look at how social discomfort, awkwardness, and weirdness are often built into the dynamics of social interactions.

There are a lot of open questions involved in any conversation, whether with a friend or a stranger, one-on-one or in a group:

- Who initiates?
- How do you initiate?
- If the other person asks, "How's it going?" what answer do you want to give? Especially since a too personal or too vague (or, in my case, too abstract) answer can make it hard for the other person to engage, thus sapping momentum from the conversation.
- What do you do when you run out of steam or topics?

---

79 American Psychiatric Association. (2013). Social Anxiety Disorder. In *Diagnostic and Statistical Manual of Mental Disorders* (5th ed.).

- If you're talking to a person at a group gathering, how do you know when they want to move on? How do you know when *you're* ready to move on? And, of course, how do you smoothly move on?
- If it's a group conversation at a gathering, what do you do when the conversation loses steam for everyone? (If you're at a meal, *please don't* make a comment about how everyone must be enjoying their food—that's so awkward!)

All of the above can cause a painful "*This* is awkward and overwhelming!" feeling, but it's important not to always translate that into "*I'm* so awkward!" As a therapist explained to me once, blaming yourself implies that responsibility for social smoothness is entirely yours, which is unrealistic and unfair. Conversational chemistry (or lack thereof) reflects on *all participants.*

For handling or preventing social awkwardness, specifically in a party-like environment, here's what I recommend:

1. Have a game plan! This means deciding before the party whether you want to work up the energy to approach strangers. It means thinking ahead about knowing what you want from your time with others. You can take a moment to consider what you'd like to share or discuss so you're ready for the "What's up?" question. Similarly, you can think about what you hope to ask others to be friendly, initiate rather than wait for them to do it, and get into a conversation you might find rewarding. The key factor here is that *you're focused on what you want and whom you'll like* rather than whether others will like you.
2. Blame the other at least some of the time. If the conversation lacks momentum and isn't rewarding, maybe it's because the other person isn't that interesting to you! Instead of thinking, *I don't know what to do with myself, so I must be the awkward one,* try to think, *This conversation isn't really drawing me in, so I guess it's generally awkward to be here,* or even just, *This isn't my kind of person.* You're

154

not necessarily judging yourself or them; you're simply taking note that you don't have much conversational chemistry.

3. Let the sensations of social discomfort wash over and past you. These feelings are very similar to those of embarrassment, which makes it very easy to blame yourself. It's easy to turn sensations into interpretations: *I feel weird, so I must be doing something weird.* If you can treat the sensations as sensations (and not turn them into interpretive stories), you won't get caught up in the blame game.

It's not just you—socializing is weird! So don't be too hard on yourself.

From Gaslighting
to Intersubjectivity:
How to Stop Driving
Each Other Crazy

Crazy-making? Yes. Gaslighting? No.

Gaslight is the title of two 1940[80]/1944[81] movies (same plot device, different adaptations of the play[82]) in which a criminal husband makes his wife question her own sanity, most notably by making the gaslights flicker and then denying it. In its original context, then, gaslighting means intentionally making someone feel like they're going crazy . . . by knowingly and maliciously denying reality.

However, in its modern context, the word's meaning has been expanded. People apply it to *any* situation in which someone else's words or behaviors make them question their sense of reality. This expansion is problematic because it paints all crazy-making situations with the same brush. It requires us to interpret all crazy-making situations by casting at least one participant's intent and behavior as abusive. This leads us to fail to recognize and respond appropriately to crazy-making situations between honest and well-meaning actors. There's a distinction to be made here that will help us treat each other a lot better.

80 Dickinson, T. (Director). (June 25, 1940). *Gaslight* [Film]. British National Films.
81 Cukor, G. (Director). (May 4, 1944). *Gaslight* [Film]. Metro-Goldwyn-Mayer.
82 Hamilton, P. *Gas Light*. Premiered December 5, 1938.

So, what's that distinction? Classic gaslighting is done intentionally, knowingly, and maliciously. The classic gaslighter wants the other person to feel crazy; they know what's real and what isn't, and they are denying this reality (a.k.a. lying) to dominate the other person. But in the expanded use, the alleged gaslighter isn't necessarily aware that they are gaslighting. Nor are they necessarily trying to hurt the other.

Why does the distinction matter? Consider this example, in which two people genuinely remember a conversation differently:

- A: "You said it's sunny!"
- B: "I didn't say that. I said it's cloudy!"

Is B gaslighting A? It certainly looks that way since B is denying A's memory. But imagine the same conversation flipped:

- B: "I said it's cloudy!"
- A: "You didn't say that. You said it's sunny!"

In the second dialogue, A is denying B, so . . . does that mean A is now the gaslighter instead? Is the gaslighter just whoever disagrees and happens to speak second? This can't be right. What if each of them truly has a different memory of the conversation in question? If each is sincerely arguing for their own memory, it's cynical to accuse either of them of gaslighting and nonsensical to accuse them both.

And yet, if we're sincerely arguing about what happened, we are each asserting or defending our own reality, *a side effect of which is denying the other's reality.* Each one can feel "gaslit" (made to question their reality by a liar intending to make them question their reality) without anyone doing the gaslighting. And because we feel that way, we accuse the other, and any further discussion is cut short. We've shut down any possibility of navigating and negotiating our seemingly competing realities. We use the accusation "Gaslighter!" to claim the moral high ground and put the "gaslighter" in their place.

Yes, it's crazy-making. No, it's not on purpose. And frankly, you're both driving the other crazy because you're arguing from different subjective realities.

What we have here is not gaslighting. *It's a failure of intersubjectivity.*

What Is Intersubjectivity?

Oh, *intersubjectivity*, I want to spread you far and wide. Why must you have so many syllables? Why must you be so abstract? It'll never take off as #intersubjectivity, but it should. Intersubjectivity holds the key to driving each other a bit less crazy.

The basic definition of *intersubjectivity* is "the relation or intersection between people's points of view."[83] That's the descriptive version: *inter*, meaning "between," and *subjectivity*, meaning "people's points of view." (While *intersubjectivity* is certainly a mouthful, it's faster than saying the full definition, so that's something. Give this unwieldy word a chance!)

For my purposes, I'm treating *intersubjectivity* as something to prescribe, so I'll define it as the following:

*A set of practices through which
people with differing points of view
don't drive each other crazy*

In my use, intersubjectivity is a value or something to aspire to. As a value, intersubjectivity is about relationships, not about truth. It doesn't require you to deny actual[84] truth but to recognize that getting along with each other requires a virtuous humility about your own sense of reality and curiosity about the other's.

---

83 Intersubjectivity. (2024, August 31). In Wikipedia. https://en.wikipedia.org/wiki/Intersubjectivity
84 Sometimes called "objective."

Beliefs and Practices for Fostering Intersubjectivity

1. Foster your own subjectivity.

Before you can encounter another's point of view, you'll need to flesh out your own. What's your version of "How it went"? What are the particular details of your interactions that stuck out to you and led to your interpretation of events? What meaning do you take or make from your interactions, and why do they matter to you?

This practice is important because it puts you in a reflective state of mind, giving you a chance to see how your own point of view is constructed from your history, social position, experiences, and emotional responses. Hopefully, this practice gives you pause when you consider the other's perspective. Maybe their interpretations and responses *also* come from an authentic personal experience with deep roots. Be curious: Is your friend truly overreacting, or are they having an appropriate reaction given their history? What could they have been through that led them to take their position?

2. Honor the other's subjectivity.

It's on you to wonder and work to piece together the other's perspective, what stands out to them, and why it matters. Even if they are indeed in the wrong (their version is *not* what happened), they are coming by their perspective honestly. It, too, is a product of their history, social position, experiences, emotional responses, and more. Their arguments are motivated by an intense need to assert their own reality (something you can relate to!), not simply to deny yours.

To honor another's subjectivity requires reaching out to understand them, how they came to have their perspective, and what it means to them. Even a false memory is an expression of the feeling they had during and after the interaction; you should see how they feel, then reflect[85] that back to them, even if you see it and feel it otherwise.

---

85 A fancy therapist word for "demonstrating understanding."

You should read and respond to the other charitably to allow for the possibility that, even though they are wrong, they truly believe they are right. They are having an honest emotion based on an incorrect assumption. You can understand their wrongness as just that—they're wrong, and it's a problem. But it's not gaslighting.

3. Break the cycle of shutting each other down.

Before we go further, a word about truth: Intersubjectivity is not a form of relativism. You don't have to believe, "Well, everyone is right in their own way." On the contrary, we all have the capacity to be mistaken, incorrect, and wrong. In fact, intersubjectivity[86] is not a statement about truth at all; it's the belief that our relationships depend on a shared desire to understand each other and honor the sincerity we each bring to the argument.

How do you break the cycle then?

By speaking for the overall dilemma. Not just your side of it. What does this sound like? "Hmmm, we keep going back and forth, and that might be because we're each holding only a piece of the whole situation. We're each showing up with our own perspectives and needs, and we're not going to get further unless we coordinate them better. I need to understand how you came to your perspective." A quotation attributed to Abraham Lincoln expresses the sentiment here: "I do not like that person. I must get to know him [*sic*] better."

Do You Still Get to Judge People Though?

You sure do! Judge each other by how hard and how well they work to foster intersubjectivity with one another.

Now we've changed the accusation—instead of saying, "They are gaslighting me," say, "They're not showing that they care about intersubjectivity." You can see the other as so wrapped up in their

---

86 As I'm using it.

own perspective that all they can do is insist on it rather than opening themselves to the other's meaning.

This new accusation is more useful because it raises two new questions: (1) Well, what am I doing to foster intersubjectivity here? (2) What would I like them to do to foster intersubjectivity here? Answering these questions leads to more collaborative requests. We've replaced "Stop gaslighting me!" with "I need us to take a step back and notice how we're seeing and talking past each other."

I'll end with two important notes:

- Classic gaslighting does indeed exist. I'm not saying it doesn't. I just think we shouldn't confuse it with failures of intersubjectivity.
- Fostering intersubjectivity can be really hard! A high amount of emotional intelligence and communication skills are required on all sides. In the next essay, I'll provide an introduction to the therapeutic standard for practicing intersubjectivity—the process conversation.

Spread the word! #intersubjectivity

Process Conversations: How to Practice Intersubjectivity Together

It's easy to get along when everyone's getting along. We're drawn to each other by all the good things, the good times, and how good it feels to be around each other. But the strength of a relationship depends on the quality of its conflicts. If your conflicts escalate, spiral, explode, seethe, and compound, and they do so repeatedly, no amount of good times make up for them. Arguments turn into wars. It's so easy to drive each other crazy and be driven apart.

But how the heck do you disagree without driving each other crazy?

By having process conversations—conversations in which you step back from the argument, try to understand what's making it more intense, and identify what each of you can do to make it less antagonistic. In the previous essay, I referred to this as fostering #intersubjectivity—a fancy word that really should have gone viral by now—ways of working collaboratively with other people in all of their otherness.

You need to always keep in mind that the other is truly other. You can try to imagine what they think, why they do what they do, what they'd like you to do . . . but you can't actually know anything unless they tell you. A process conversation lives and dies according to how well each of us can remain open, curious, and humble with each other. You're always better off assuming you don't understand rather than reacting quickly to every perceived insult.

In this essay, I'd like to share six major steps involved in having process conversations. When both people are committed to using these steps (and possibly some more personalized instructions from your therapist), you will have more pleasant and more productive arguments. The goal is to have the kind of difficult conversations that end with both folks saying, "I'm really glad we talked about this. Thank you!"

Here are the steps:

1. Foster subjectivity.
2. Want a process conversation and then initiate one.
3. Sleuth together.
4. Agree on semantics.
5. Offer (and counteroffer) potential solutions.
6. Agree to return and discuss as needed.

Numbers 3, 4, and 5 all depend on skills for identifying and breaking feedback loops, which I'll introduce before moving on to them.

Fostering Subjectivity

Before you can be open to the other's reality, you need to be in touch with your own. You need to be ready to speak for yourself. And you'll do a much better job if you've done some reflection in advance. Here are some questions for clarifying your own position:

- What is bothering you right now in this relationship?
- What are they doing that bothers you?
- Why are you bothered by it?
- What are the various feelings you're having about all of this?
- Does the situation and/or the person remind you of earlier situations/people you've encountered? Does it set off any particularly raw feelings in you?[87]

---

87 Buster Benson, *Why Are We Yelling? The Art of Productive Disagreement.* (Portfolio, 2019).

- What's your story about why they're doing it?
- How would you describe the play-by-play interactions in this conflict?
- Finally, what do you think *they* would say about your situation? (What's bothering them, why, etc.)

These questions help you organize and verbalize your perspective and begin to imagine the other's. All this preparation will improve your own readiness to express yourself and be open to them in the actual conversation.

Wanting a Process Conversation and Initiating

How you initiate the conversation will be shaped by what you want out of it, which is why I've combined these two steps. If you want to give them a piece of your mind, you're more likely to make a strong approach, accusing and attacking, which sets the tone for a fight. You may have fantasies about ranting at the other person, a.k.a. letting them have it. It's a satisfying fantasy to have but an unsatisfying way to approach a difficult conversation. Why? Because it never takes into account the possibility that the other person might respond with their own accusations and attacks. You make a plan to drop truth bombs on someone, never imagining that they might have their own arsenal. And each of you fails to realize that attacking is how you start a war, not cultivate peace.

But first, you won't initiate a process conversation unless you realize you want one. What would motivate you to want a process conversation? You'll need to start with some essential assumptions:

- You care about this relationship and improving your ability to connect when there's conflict.
- You don't know the full story of what's going on between the two of you.

- You are most likely[88] both contributing to the conflict—you're setting each other off.
- You cannot singlehandedly solve this issue.

If you want to figure out the issue but can't know fully what's going on, you'll need to enlist the other person's help. You can sit around and ask (rhetorically), *What were they thinking?* But instead, you need to truly wonder, *Hmm, what were they actually thinking?* A process conversation requires an authentic desire to understand their perspective. You need to assume that you're missing a piece of the puzzle and your stories about (and solutions to) the conflict will be incomplete.

Driven by this curiosity, your initiation will be curious as well:

- Our conversations keep turning into arguments. What's going on between us?
- Will you help me figure out how this is happening?
- Can we compare perspectives on why and how these conversations are spiraling?

A Preliminary Note About Feedback Loops

The steps involving sleuthing, semantics, and solutions will require an understanding of feedback loops and how to interrupt them.

In a feedback loop, one thing leads to another. A heated argument is filled with positive feedback loops. Despite the word *positive*, this is actually a bad thing, as escalation leads to further escalation, with each person trying to one-up the other. The attacks pile on, and the problem grows bigger. A negative feedback loop keeps this from happening. Instead of piling on, you can pull back, check in, and slow your responses —all of which hopefully serve to cool down the conversation for both of

---

88 While the maxim in couples counseling is that the problem is the couples' patterns of interacting, I maintain a "monster exception" to this rule—in some relationships, one person is simply a "monster" (think abusive). The responsibility is not always equally distributed.

you. A negative feedback loop is thus more productive than a positive feedback loop.

Here's the key insight into creating productive feedback loops: *The power to escalate or de-escalate lies in how you respond to one another.* Think of a conversation as a series of initiations and responses, remembering that each response is then an initiation to the next response. You have limited power to get it right the first time, to express your thoughts and feelings in a way that makes you 100 percent sure the other will take it well. Even the most tactful of approaches will fail to satisfy someone inclined to respond reactively and defensively.

This is where negative feedback comes in. You don't have to react with "How dare you?" You can respond with, "Saying it like that really rubs me the wrong way. Is there another way you can say it?" You can tell the other person how you feel instead of throwing the feeling at them. You can make a request instead of a counterattack.

Now, instead of having to figure out the perfect way to say something, you can focus on how each of you can respond graciously and collaboratively.

Sleuthing Together

By starting with curiosity, you two now have a shared project: piecing together the play-by-play of the conflict. How are you setting each other off? What are the moves and countermoves by which you turn a problem into a bigger one?

You piece it together by comparing notes and following the classic formula of IFWY statements: "I feel ___ when you ___."

Pretty much every self-help article on this topic encourages IFWY statements, but it's usually for the purpose of sharing what you feel without making the other person feel attacked. This is all well and good, but after you've said your piece, what exactly should the other person do with this information? What response will lead the conversation forward?

To me, IFWY statements are how you play detective together and construct a shared story of how the fight is taking its course. Every

IFWY statement connects two more dots. You can make a chain of them, seeing how each action sets off a feeling and each feeling sets off an action.

Here's why this distinction matters. Without an understanding of what to do with them, you can still use IFWYs to fight and escalate:

- A: "I feel ___ when you ___!"
- B: "Oh yeah, well, I feel ___ when you ___!"
- A: "Oh yeah, well, *I* wouldn't ___ if *you* didn't ___."

In the version above, you're using IFWYs to blame the other for your feelings and actions, arguing about whose actions were justified and whose were blameworthy.

In my version, we see each other's IFWY as important pieces of the puzzle:

- A: "I feel ___ when you ___!"
- B: "Oh, huh. I see how that works. Right. But then you do something with that feeling, and then I feel ___ when you ___!"
- A: "Right, right. You do this, and so I do that, and so you do this other thing, and that's how we end up here."
- B: "Yep."

Of course, you sometimes don't understand why they feel that way, and your own lack of understanding can easily lead you to slip into thinking that their feelings and actions make no sense in general. Then you end up saying something like "Well, you shouldn't feel that way!" This derails the conversation. When you don't understand, you should name it:

- A: "I feel ___ when you ___!"
- B: "I don't understand. What are you saying I'm doing? And how does it lead to your feeling that? I'm sorry. I believe you make sense, but I'm not getting it yet."

One common snag in the exchange of IFWYs is arguing about the roles of intentions and impact. Both are important, but folks often try to use one to discount the other:

- A: "IFWY."
- B: "I know I did that, but you're taking it the wrong way! You need to appreciate my intentions. Then you won't feel bad about what I did."
- A: "Yes, but IFWY. Stop hiding behind your intentions as if they make what you said/did okay."

Both intentions and impact are important. You both need to acknowledge both. Otherwise, you'll just go in circles, arguing about which matters more.

Agreeing on Semantics

The next common snag in an argument is disagreeing over semantics, or the meaning of your words. And here's the one I hear the most:

- A: "Stop yelling at me!"
- B: "I'm not yelling!"

You won't need to argue over semantics if you can just negotiate about them. You can do this by developing working definitions (agreeing to use a term in a specific way, regardless of its dictionary definition) or developing linguistic granularity (getting more detailed in how you describe something). Here's what that might sound like:

- A: "Stop yelling at me!"
- B: "Hold on, I don't think of this as yelling because, to me, yelling is about getting loud, and I'm not getting loud."
- A: "Hmm . . . Right, you're not getting loud, but you are getting sarcastic/name-calling/making accusations/et cetera. You're using a calm voice, but it's still upsetting."
- B: "Okay, I can see that. I'm not yelling, but I am doing that."

You won't get stuck on words if you can remain curious about what the other means by them. What you mean by a word matters more than the word itself, so get clear on your meanings. Then you're free to move on.

A related snag—hearing the other person say something offensive or seemingly offensive and immediately reacting rather than being curious. In this instance, it is *very* hard not to be reactive. And yet, if you can remain curious, the conversation is less likely to get derailed. Try to foster confusion instead of outrage:

- "What did you mean by that?"
- "When you say it that way, here's what I'm hearing."

Hopefully, questions like this prompt the other person to think about their intention vs. their impact and give them a chance to restate what they said. "Oh, I'm definitely not trying to come off that way, but I can see how I would be. Let me try it again."

Offering (and Counteroffering) Potential Solutions

Now that you have a shared understanding of the play-by-play in your arguments—how discussions escalate into full-blown arguments—the final task is to brainstorm and try out ways to de-escalate the argument through a productive practice of pitching and responding to potential solutions.

Pitching will take the form of what-if questions. "Instead of saying/doing it this way, what if I/you . . .?" In this process, I strongly recommend making offers about what you'll do differently rather than telling them what to do differently. An offer is more collaborative than a request, especially since requests can often be heard as veiled commands. Of course, if the other person asks for ideas about what they can do differently, go for it.

Before I describe some general potential solutions, let's spell out how the rhythm of offer and counteroffer works. If you like their offer, hooray! Move on to the following step. But if you don't like their offer, you need to practice mindful responses. Here's how that goes poorly:

- A: "Okay, so what if I . . .?"
- B: "That's a terrible idea. Nope, we're not doing that." (Rejecting response)
- A: "Well, what the hell then? I guess I just won't even bother trying." (Feeling rejected, giving up)

Instead, the offer/counteroffer process is about workshopping, tweaking, amending, and troubleshooting:

- A: "Okay, so what if I . . .?"
- B: "Interesting. But this part of it doesn't work for me because . . . What if we altered that part to . . . instead?"
- A: "I see how that's better. But here's how it doesn't quite work for me. What if we . . . ? (And so on)

In regard to generating potential solutions, I can offer only some basic ideas since relational conflicts can be so unique to the participants.[89] Here are a few thoughts:

1. In analyzing and improving the language you use, focus on the types of communication. Respectful communication is really hard to get right; it's much easier to fall back on passive, aggressive, and passive-aggressive communication. You'll have to try out different lines on each other to see what comes off sounding respectful. It's really tricky!
2. Think outside the box, using what I call "the fictional approach." In fiction, anything goes, and that's a great way to start brainstorming.

---

89 Tolstoy, L. (1995). *Anna Karenina* (A. Maude & L. Maude, Trans.). Wordsworth Editions. Page 1.

To take turns during a conversation, what if you use a conch?[90] Would it help to answer questions with questions?[91] What would Homer Simpson do? What would Yoda do? Even if this approach generates some truly bad ideas, those can always be the beginning of offer/counteroffer negotiations.

3. One way of de-escalating, if done well, is to initiate a temporary break from the discussion. If you get heated, give yourselves a chance to cool down. A pause is one of the best ways to de-escalate, but initiating it can be done poorly. I can't stand how often people on TV simply march out of the room (sometimes loudly) as a way of ending a conversation. It's okay to leave, but it would be better if they just said, "I need to take a break. Let's return to this when I've cooled down!" Now their marching out has a relation-positive context. The person left behind knows that the other one left for the sake of improving communication and plans to come back. The person left behind will feel less abandoned. Folks might signal that they need a break by using some agreed-upon language (a safe word, if you will), even something as simple as "Pause."[92]

Agreeing to Return and Discuss as Needed

If you come up with some shared resolutions, cool! Go try them out and see how they work. If they do, hooray! If not . . . it sounds like you'll have to get together to sleuth and solve again. The possibility of reopening the conversation should always be part of the resolution. By recognizing that discussions and plans can be incomplete, you avoid the pitfall of blaming one another for the failure of the plan. At all costs, you shouldn't be setting yourselves up to say, "Hey, I thought we talked about this!"—a line that has implied accusations. ("*We* had a great plan, but *you* failed to follow it.") Instead, try this: "Darn. I thought we had a

---

90 Golding, William, 1911-1993. (1954). *Lord of the Flies*. New York: Perigee, 1954.
91 Stoppard, T. (1994). *Rosencrantz & Guildenstern Are Dead*. Atlantic Books.
92 *How I Met Your Mother*, "Unpause" (Season 9, Episode 15), 2014.

good plan, but I guess it needs more work. Can we come up with some other ideas to try out?"

Conclusion

It's a lot, isn't it? It's amazing that anyone gets along at all, given that there are just *so* many ways to fight poorly. Start slowly. Read this essay together and check to see how each of you understands it and feels about it. Heck, you can have a process conversation about process conversations.

"Okay, Matt says do this. But what if we do this . . .?" Try out each step, work on your skills, and agree to keep working on this. Together, collaboratively and carefully, you can spiral upward.

USE THERAPY TO FIND YOUR WAY

"Psychotherapy is not a substitute for life but a dress rehearsal for life. In other words, though psychotherapy requires a close relationship, the relationship is not an end - it is a means to an end."

— Irvin Yalom

"Therapy's like going to the gym."

—Chris Pine

You've been wandering through life for a while, and now your energy, your strength, and your spirit are waning. You need sustenance and wisdom, and you're not finding enough of it here. You're wondering whether you need to look somewhere new. But how to get there? What exactly are you looking for, and how will you recognize it? What if you find something but it's the wrong thing? What do you need to take with you on your journey? How will you take your findings back out with you, and how will you use them?

You're in the forest of psychotherapy. The *mushrooms* are therapists and their methods, insights, and recommendations. You are a hungry forager. You want to find the edible mushrooms and avoid the poisonous ones, take them home with you, process them, eat them, and maybe go back to the forest for more.

Mushroom hunting is an exciting and dangerous endeavor. You're best served by researching before you start—checking your pantry to see what's missing and consulting with guides about what you're looking for and where to look. Some species grow only on certain trees or in certain regions. Going out into the forest is an adventure that comes with risks and benefits. You may or may not find what you're looking for, and you'll need focus, vigilance, and plenty of patience.

Once you've found some mushrooms, you'll need to analyze them and try to determine if they are edible or poisonous. There are a lot of characteristics you can use for identification—size, coloring, cap and stem shapes, gills, texture, cross section, and spore print. Some mushrooms are boring, typical, and edible; others are boring, typical, and poisonous. Not all mushrooms are poisonous to every animal. The edible ones and the poisonous ones can look almost identical. This might sound overwhelming, but the more you do it, the more you learn about what you're looking for and more quickly tell them apart. It's best to avoid ingesting a poisonous mushroom. But if you do, you can usually tell based on gastrointestinal distress—then seek medical treatment!

Mushrooms are pretty fascinating organisms. Well, specifically, they are the fruits of *underground* organisms that are connected by a root network. Where you find one mushroom, you should look for others like it close by. Because the organism is underground, they are known to pop up quickly and seemingly out of nowhere, a.k.a. mushrooming. Some pop up quickly and remain; others might grow rapidly but then disappear quickly; others grow quite slowly.

Mushroom foraging is not about moving into the forest but rather making excursions into the forest, getting what you need, and returning home. You'll need a knife to cut out the mushroom and a brush to wipe off debris. Out of the forest, you can take steps to enhance their nutritional value. Exposing the mushrooms to sunlight increases vitamin D. Cooking them aids digestion. And, if you know what you're doing, you can use the mushroom spores to grow your own at home!

Psychotherapy is an exciting and dangerous endeavor. You're best served by doing some personal reflection and learning before you start looking. What kind of change do you need? What kind of therapy offers what kind of change? And where the heck does one start in finding a therapist? Finding a therapist—one you like—can take some time and include a number of false starts. It will take focus, vigilance, and plenty of patience.

Even if you have found a promising therapist, it can still take some time to confirm that you two are a good or bad fit. A lot of therapists and types of therapy can look and feel the same. Some might work well for others but not for you. The more you look and check with yourself about how it's going, the better you'll get at finding what works for you. Unfortunately, you might learn only by noticing that your symptoms are getting worse. Fortunately, the effects of bad therapy are usually less immediately fatal than a poisonous mushroom. Either way, looking for a new provider (or medical attention) is a good move.

Therapists and therapeutic insights are fascinating organisms, as the fruits emerge out of extensive underground roots. Where you find one therapeutic insight, you should look for others like it close by. Some insights can seemingly pop up out of nowhere; if you're not vigilant, some can disappear just as quickly. Other insights grow slowly.

Unless you are experiencing acute mental illness, therapy is not about moving in with your therapist but rather entering a therapy session, getting what you need, and returning home. Bring a notepad to jot down insights to take home with you. Bring your best judgment to remove the unnecessary or unpleasant aspects of your therapist's input—a.k.a. "Take what you need and leave the rest." Most importantly, process your therapeutic experiences by continuing to reflect on them between sessions and practicing any new insights and habits to truly absorb their therapeutic value. And, if you know what you're doing, you can reflect on the therapeutic process and generate some of your own insights at home!

The essays in this section will help you get the most out of your therapy experience—finding and vetting therapists, preparing and starting sessions, engaging actively in therapeutic dialogue, and using insights and recommendations for greater satisfaction in life.

Ten Ways to Tell if Your Therapist Honors Consent (And Why That Matters)

Ideally, your therapist is knowledgeable, effective, and committed to your growth and healing. But! No therapist is all-knowing, all-powerful, or all-good—so watch out if they seem to think they are. Just as your therapist should help cultivate your sense of power in life, so should they cultivate a sense of your power during sessions. *They* work for *you*.

How can you tell if your therapist respects your power as a client? It's all about **consent-seeking**, which in a therapist looks like (1) checking for understanding, (2) providing transparency about their intentions, and (3) getting permission before making an intervention[93].

Checking for Understanding

1. "Before giving their feedback, does my therapist make sure they understand what I just said?"

It's cheap for someone to say, "I hear you," or "I get it," and then move on to making their own point. A better practice is for them to say what they heard, then check with you to see if *you* think they get it.

---

93 In the therapy world, *intervention* is jargon for any action taken with therapeutic intent.

2.   "Does my therapist ever tell me they can relate to what I'm saying?"

This kind of reassurance can feel supportive, but it can also be dangerous territory. They might be relating . . . or they might wrongly be assuming that their experience is identical to yours and that their personal solutions will work just as well for you. Insist that they check for understanding. What exactly are they relating to? Can they express any humility, any openness to the possibility that their relating might be entirely about themselves?

I love to use this line with clients: "I think I'm relating, but I might just be projecting. I'll tell you what I'm thinking, and you'll tell me if it's true for you or if I'm just talking about myself." A line like this gives them the opportunity to confirm, deny, or modify what I said. No matter what their response, I'm now closer to understanding, and they are closer to feeling understood.

3.   "Does my therapist respect my choice of therapeutic topics and agendas?"

If it feels like they're changing the subject or taking the conversation in their own direction, name it and ask them about their intentions. You can say, "I want to talk about X, but you just brought up Y. I'm curious about how you're connecting those two things."

A consent-oriented therapist will keep the focus where you want it to be. If they want to introduce a topic or direction, they'll name that they're bringing in something new, provide a meaningful explanation for how their proposed topic or agenda serves yours, and ask if you think it's worth pursuing. If they didn't provide an explanation in advance, they will be glad and grateful that you prompted them. (For more on therapeutic topics and agendas, see "How to Prepare for a Therapy Session" on page 183.)

4.   A question for yourself after the session: "Do I feel understood?"

How can you tell if you feel understood? You'll know if you come away feeling like you make sense—that your experiences and responses to those experiences make sense. Coming out of a therapy session, you will hopefully be feeling this: "Okay! I'm human. I'm troubled. I'm going through a hard time, but I'm human. It makes sense to struggle with what I'm going through." If you leave the session with that feeling, it likely indicates that the therapist felt that way about you as well and communicated it effectively.

Transparency About Their Intentions

5. "Has my therapist explained their approach to therapy and personal change, and does it appeal to me?"

Like with any group project, a shared plan is essential for success. If you don't know their process for therapy, there's no real way to give consent. So, you might ask them about their understanding of how mental health issues and symptoms arise. How do they believe personal growth and healing happen? What therapeutic methods do they use, and what's the power in them? (For more, see "Start Process Conversations with Your Therapist" on page 213.)

How will you know if their approach appeals to you? (1) If it makes sense and you feel like you now have somewhat of a road map to the change you want; and (2) It gives you a feeling of hope, if not excitement.

6. "During the session, if my therapist offers an interpretation or suggestion, do they (can they) explain how it works and why they think it will be helpful? Or does it feel like my therapist is pulling moves on me?"

A therapist can be very helpful by offering a path toward growth and healing, then assisting with each step of the way. But they shouldn't trick you into that path or lead you in a direction without explaining where it's going.

One type of therapeutic move is to intentionally overstate a point to provoke a response. For example, you are talking about a fight with a friend and getting rather animated, but you're not talking about your emotions. Your therapist might say, "Wow, you really hate them!" Hearing such an exaggerated (and probably wrong) reflection, you'll feel a need to correct them by clarifying how you feel and providing more nuance than they did.

It's a fascinating move that can be quite effective . . . except that it works through manipulation! The therapist is playing dumb, intentionally getting it wrong, to trick you into telling your truth. But, to me, just a touch of transparency makes this move perfectly fine. When I want to pull a move like this, I say, "Okay, I'm gonna say something kinda extreme, but I don't believe it. I'm just saying it to see how you'll respond." Instead of pulling a move, we're now playing a game, and the client is now in on it.

7.   A question for yourself after the session: "If the session felt challenging, did my therapist make it clear why these challenges were necessary?"

Therapy can be a psychological workout, and when it comes to working out, people like to say, "No pain, no gain." This is often true . . . except there is such a thing as pain without gain.[94] If you're leaving sessions feeling like a total mess, it might indicate that the therapist is not preparing you adequately for the intervention or that they are using an intervention not suited to your needs. Conversing (before and after) about the intervention puts both of you on the same page and gives you the power to address concerns about it.

Getting Permission Before an Intervention

8.   "If I share questions or doubts about what they're saying, do they respond graciously?"

You don't owe them unconditional faith and obedience. Trust a therapist only if they respond well to corrections, questions, and challenges.

---

94 Try dead-lifting with your back instead of your legs (Do NOT actually try this!) and you'll see what I'm talking about.

What does responding well look like? What it doesn't look like: getting defensive, attacking you, or saying, "Just trust me.[95]" What it does look like: seeking to understand your feedback, then integrating your feedback into what they are saying and doing.

9. "If they keep giving me the same interpretations or interventions, does it still feel like a friendly and collaborative conversation, or do I feel pushed around?"

A therapist with a specific therapeutic approach can be a very good resource. Through their professional, reflective, and caring lens, they may see something you don't—a novel way of understanding and approaching situations in life. Because their approach is new to you, it may require some persistence on their end to make an impact.

On the other hand, they might just have an obsession with a particular approach, be stuck in it, and be unable to get past it to meet you where you are.[96] But, whether their approach is useful or not, they need to be interested in making that connection with you, justify their approach, be open to your challenges, and build a collaborative relationship.

It's a good thing for your therapist to feel confident, as it can be demoralizing to work with someone who's too wishy-washy. At the same time, humility is essential—you shouldn't feel like you are being bullied into adopting *their* approach to *your* life.

10. A question for yourself after the session: "Am I glad I went to this session?"

Because it's a workout focused on your emotional life, it's a little weird to say that therapy can be enjoyable. But the fact is, it really can be! The thought *Wow, that was hard, but I enjoy working with them!* can be a good sign that you have a power-sharing, consent-oriented therapist.

---

95 Or this variation: "I've been in the field for a long time; I know what I'm doing."
96 A "fun" example: The week after I read *The Angry Book*, I was convinced that every one of my clients was having anger issues. Rubin, T. I. (1970). *The Angry Book*. Collier.

Conclusion

Doesn't consent-oriented therapy sound nice? To have a therapist who feels powerful but not to the detriment of your own power? I wish this for you. You don't have to settle for less.

How to Prepare for
a Therapy Session

You Don't Have to Prepare

First of all, you don't have to prepare. It's not a class, job interview, or dance recital. I start all my sessions by asking, "What would you like to do today?" Most of my clients (most of the time) respond with "I don't know." Yet most of our sessions end up being productive anyhow. When they say, "I don't know," I invite them to think, review their recent experiences, or review (or make me review) our recent sessions. Then we go from there.

Some people even *prefer* to show up unprepared. They might feel this way because they find the improvisation of self-exploration more liberating and productive, or they prefer therapy to be a closed container—a place to pick up and then leave intimate issues, which frees them not to ruminate on those issues the rest of the week.

But If You Want To . . .

But! Maybe you'd like to prepare? If you want to get something specific out of a therapy session, you're more likely to get it (and maybe even get it faster) by showing up prepared for your therapy session.

To prepare for a session, I recommend first scanning yourself for **topics**, from which you can then start identifying **agendas**. A topic is just a subject of interest; an agenda is what you'd like to do with the topic in therapy.

Topics

First, scan yourself for topics. Either something comes to mind immediately or you can ask yourself really broad questions, like:

- "What have I been up to?"
- "What's been going on?"
- "What's been bothering me?"
- "When my mind wanders, or when I'm alone with my thoughts, what have I been thinking about?"

Whatever comes to mind, those are all possible topics. It's okay to come in with just a topic and no agenda. You can come in with a vague sense that this is something worth talking, thinking, or feeling about, and together you'll see where that goes.

Agendas

The next step is to identify any therapeutic agenda you have regarding the topic(s). Very generally, there are three therapeutic agendas:

- Venting/sharing: "I need to get this [topic] off my chest!"
- Exploring: "I need to figure out what is up with me and this [topic]!"
- Planning: "I need to figure out what to do with this [topic]!"

The exclamation points above are significant—you identify therapeutic topics and agendas by noticing what seems to have emotional force when they come to mind. It's helpful to show up at the restaurant hungry and with an appetite; in therapy, it's helpful to show up with an issue and a desire to address that issue.

If you want to find an agenda before arriving, I recommend journaling, talking to someone else, or talking aloud to yourself about the topic. Pay attention to where your train of thought starts going in loops or hitting walls. Pay attention to where your emotions (including physical sensations related to emotion) spike, swell, or even get in the way of thinking. When you notice where you hit loops, walls, and other forms of psychological turmoil, two questions will likely come to mind: (1) "What the heck is going on?" (2) "What the heck can I do with it?" You've found your agenda.

When to Prepare

Most of the time, if a client does show up with a topic and agenda, it's something they thought of on their way to the session or while sitting in the (real or virtual) waiting room. That's fine!

If you want to prepare earlier than that, consider doing some writing about your topic and agenda. (I'm a big fan of making lists; it's way easier than writing in paragraphs.) You might do the following:

- First, write out the important details of the topic.
- Then list your various thoughts, feelings, ideas for action, etc., that arise when you try to focus on the topic.
- Finally, try to recognize when your reflections are hitting walls or loops, and ask yourself why. It even helps to ask yourself (compassionately, not sarcastically), "What is so hard about this?"

You can do this the night before the session or even the morning of. Some folks find it helpful to keep a running list of topics and agendas that come to mind as they are going about their day or week. I definitely recommend this. It's a bummer when clients come in saying, "I totally had an important thing I wanted to discuss and work on, but I can't remember what it was." As a client myself, I keep a running list on my phone, as it's usually more immediately available than paper and pen.

Finally, for the real overachievers (guilty as charged), preparation for the next session can begin as soon as you step out of the previous session. I voice-dictate an email to myself, naming the important thoughts, insights, and ideas I want to carry over into my personal reflections and pursue further at my next session.

I find that preparing in advance can help me feel less overwhelmed when I enter the session and during the week between sessions. A thought or feeling comes to mind, and I notice the inner turmoil stirred up. I do a little journaling, seeing how far I can get by thinking and feeling it out for myself. When I can't go further (whether for cognitive or emotional reasons), I stop, knowing I'll pick it up again with my therapist. It's a nice exercise to take some time to be with the feeling, then tolerate the discomfort of leaving the issue unresolved until later.

But You Don't Have To

Please consider all of the above as guidance if you're interested. If it feels overwhelming, ignore all of this. While therapy is often some hard mental and emotional work, preparing for it shouldn't stress you out.

How to Find and Vet Potential Therapists

It may be hard to realize that you (or a loved one) could benefit from therapy; it can be even harder to find a therapist! In this chapter, I provide step-by-step instructions to make your process easier and more effective. I have used this process for myself (as a client) with great success. Even before publishing this book, this chapter was the Google doc I've shared most often in my career.

Here is an overview of the sections below:

- Identify your therapeutic agenda—what do you want from therapy?
- Identify what kind of therapy you might prefer.
- Find and connect with potential therapists.
- Meet for an initial (free) consultation.
- Assess your therapist within the first one to three sessions.
- Bonus section: How to vet psychiatric medication prescribers.

Identify Your Therapeutic Agenda

You can't know if you've found something if you don't know what you're looking for! So, what's your situation, and what would you like to do with it? Or, put another way, what are your therapeutic topics, and what is your therapeutic agenda?

For extended guidance on answering these questions, see the chapter titled "How to Prepare for a Therapy Session." Once you've answered these questions, you'll be more ready to answer the first question you can expect from a therapist: "What brings you here?"

In addition to the above, I recommend making a list of symptoms you've been dealing with since the problem started. Reflect, ask people who know you, or observe yourself over a couple of days so you'll be able to speak about your:

- Mood
- Sleep
- Appetite
- Troubling thoughts
- Current life challenges or crises
- Troubling behaviors, with yourself or around others
- Other things that might answer the question "How do I know something is wrong?"

Identify What Kind of Therapy You Might Prefer

There are many types of psychotherapy and many articles already written about them.[97] It's a real mixed blessing. The information is all out there, but it's overwhelming to try to understand it all and then determine what you want for yourself. So, instead of getting an education in psychology, consider the following questions:

What are the therapist traits/actions below that appeal to you? Would you like someone who:

- Stays silent so you can unload
- Makes conversation as a way of chiming in and providing momentum/direction to the session
- Keeps their reactions hidden so their feelings don't influence you
- Makes their reactions clear so their feelings help you recognize and clarify your own
- Provides only questions so you can come to your own conclusions

97 List of Psychotherapies. (2024, August 31). In *Wikipedia*. https://en.wikipedia.org/wiki/List_of_psychotherapies

- Provides their own feedback, insights, and conclusions
- Provides education and instruction about your topic
- Uses an experiential approach (art, music, movement, mindfulness, etc.) rather than only talk therapy
- Focuses on your childhood and upbringing
- Focuses on your present
- Uses an evidence-based[98] approach
- Gives homework

Lastly: If you know what you're trying to work on, you may want to look for someone who specializes in that topic. For any given topic, there may be a gold standard treatment already—such as exposure and response prevention for obsessive-compulsive disorder (a.k.a. ERP for OCD).

Two caveats: (1) Some topics are so universal in therapy—anxiety, depression—that any therapist you look for will claim it as a specialty; and (2) There may be multiple effective approaches for a single issue (such as post-traumatic stress). So I recommend starting with some googling to find out about the various types, then be ready to shop around for the kind that feels right for you. Not every generally effective treatment will work specifically for you.

Find and Connect with Potential Therapists

Search online using a site with therapist listings, such as www.psychology today.com or www.therapyden.com. While it's helpful to google therapy types, it's not helpful to google to find therapists. It's also often unproductive to search through your insurance company's website.

---

98 "Evidence-based practice is the integration of the best available research with clinical expertise in the context of patient characteristics, culture and preferences." from American Psychological Association. (2024, August 31). *Evidence-Based Practice in Psychology.* https://www.apa.org/practice/resources/evidence

Why Search Online Through a Dedicated Site?

- Online sites make it easy to search widely and contact a lot of therapists quickly.
- Your insurance's website may not have an updated list of their approved clinicians.
- Therapists are usually busy for about fifty-three minutes out of every hour, so calling them will likely result in having to leave a message and then play phone tag. Emailing is better.
- Admittedly, I have had clients who found me through their primary care physician (PCP) or a friend's referral. These methods can also work; I just haven't used them myself.

Basic Steps

1. Write up a brief blurb about what you're looking for. See the mad lib below for a template.
2. Search through one of the websites listed above.

   - Use the filters on the left or top of the page to find only those clinicians who take your insurance.
   - Check out and use other filters on the site.
   - Click around! Take note of who appeals to you and feel free to judge based on their picture, personal description, and specialties. This is not unlike online dating, in which it's good to be selective.
   - If you want virtual therapy, anywhere in your state works—no need to search locally. If you want to meet in person, search by your town or ZIP code.

3. Use the Contact Me button on people's pages to message ten to fifteen of them. Just keep cutting and pasting your blurb each time.

Using this method, I often get several hits, request a free consultation from whoever responds, meet, and then make my selection. See below for recommendations on the consultation and selection.

Writing your Blurb: The Mad Lib

Hi, I'm [name]—[age],[gender],[relationship-status],[employment status], [any relevant diagnosis],[any mental health related medication–name, dosage, frequency].

I'm currently dealing with [name your diagnosis and/or just say "stress"] connected to [relevant life situation]. I'm seeking therapy in order to [goal].

Are you taking new clients? My insurance is [insurance]. I'm free to meet [state your availability]. I'd like to meet [in person or virtual, or say that you're flexible].

Meet for an Initial (Free) Consultation

Your potential therapist should provide (ideally, insist on) a brief consultation before agreeing to meet formally. This consultation should be free, take only about fifteen to twenty minutes, and likely take place by phone or video.

The preliminary consultation is essential for the same reasons that people date before marrying and interview before hiring—because you don't want to invest too much time, energy, and commitment just to find out you're the wrong fit. The first few actual therapy sessions are already preliminary: the intake interview can take an entire session or more, and then there are a few more sessions of just getting to know each other and testing the waters. Add to this the fact that sessions are usually scheduled weekly, and it can easily be a month or more before you know if this is a good fit. The sooner you start getting to know therapists (and filtering them out), the better.

There are three main agenda items:

1. Discuss logistics first! It doesn't matter if a therapist is a good fit if the relationship doesn't work logistically, so discuss this first and save your breath.

(a) Do they take your insurance?

(b) Does their schedule fit yours?

(c) Are they licensed in the state in which you'll see them?

(d) Are you looking for help with issues within or outside their expertise?

2. Share what motivates you to seek therapy. This step is why the initial prep (see above) is so important. You'll be ready with answers to their questions rather than fumbling around and attempting to concisely put some very intimate and complicated personal information into words for the first time.

(e) What's your situation? (Not your life story, just the basics of what's troubling you: Work? Breakup? Life changes? Mental health episode?)

(f) What are your symptoms?

(g) What are your goals for therapy?

(h) What do you think you're looking for in a therapist? (See above.)

3. They respond to you. As they respond, think about:

(i) How well do they understand or try to understand what you're saying? When they respond, do you feel like they get it?

(j) Can they explain their approach to therapy and how it works?

(k) Does their explanation make sense and appeal to you? (How do you know if it appeals to you? You may feel hope blooming inside you, and you feel like you can see a path forward; this is different from the desperate "I just need to find someone to help" feeling.)

(l) How does it feel to talk to and hear from them? Is their personality as warm, wise, confident, humble, etc., as you'd like?

Assess Your Therapist Within the First One to Three Sessions

Most of my insights here are drawn from my other chapters about consent in therapy (see "Ten Ways to Tell Your Therapist Honors Consent" on page 177) and challenging your therapist (see "It's Good to Question Your Therapist" on page 209), so this is the short version:

- Do they seem focused or distracted?
- How well do they summarize what you said?
- When they summarize, do they hit the most salient points? Or are they pointing out stuff that feels beside the point?
- Do they get defensive when you ask questions, correct them, or disagree?
- Do you feel like there's momentum or direction to the work?
- How do you feel after the sessions? Hopeful? Bummed? Please note: If you feel challenged, that can be a good or a bad thing. Yes, there's no pain, no gain, but not all pain leads to gain. Good challenge, even when hard, will also feel a little exciting. Bad challenge, even when promising, will also have a tinge of intimidation in it, as if some part of you is being forced past its limit.

After answering these questions for yourself, raise the topics with your therapist, see how they respond, then consider how you feel after that conversation.

Bonus Section! How to Vet Prescribers

1. Before the consultation, do the same prep as above, with more of a focus on listing your symptoms; that's what they'll want to know.
2. When looking, be open to both psychiatrists and psychiatric mental health nurse practitioners (PMHNP). The first kind is a doctor, but that doesn't necessarily make them a better prescriber. There are also more PMHNPs, so you're likely to get an appointment sooner if you contact them.

3. Use the guide above to find and contact one or more.
4. While meeting with them and afterward, ask yourself the following questions (in this particular order):

(1) Do they know what they're talking about?

    (a) Because they'll have more knowledge and training than you, this will be hard to tell. But you might get a sense by listening to how they explain things.

    (b) Can they speak about a variety of medications, benefits, and side effects?

(2) Are they responsive to your questions and concerns?

    (a) Responsive = Focused on understanding your needs from your perspective rather than imagining themselves in your position.[99] This is important in the initial meeting but even more so in subsequent ones while you're in the guinea pig stage of medication.

    (b) Regarding the guinea pig stage: Sorry to say, but it can take a while before you find the right medication(s) and dosage(s), and the process can be slow (while waiting for the intended effects to kick in), puzzling (are the intended effects worth the side effects?), and frustrating (I just want to feel better already!). A prescriber who seems to be using a guess-and-check method is the norm. Be sensitive to whether they are using guess-and-check in a way that honors and incorporates your feedback and concerns rather than dismissing you.

---

99 Joan B. Tronto: *Moral Boundaries. A Political Argument for an Ethic of Care.* New York, London: Routledge, 1993 (page 136).

(3) How do you feel when meeting with them?

    (a) This item is important but *far less* than the previous two. Most prescribers will not also serve as your therapist, so their expertise and responsiveness will matter much more than whether you feel any relational chemistry with them. Appointments will likely be brief and focused on symptom management, not personal exploration.

Conclusion

Good luck! There are a lot of steps, but you have to do them only one at a time. If or when it pays off, you'll be glad you did it. If this guide helps you filter out the bad-fit therapists, you'll be glad you saved yourself the time and emotional pain of forcing yourself to stay in an unhelpful relationship.

How to Start
Therapy Sessions

Therapy is a weird thing, and the beginning of sessions can be especially challenging for some people. It's awkward. You're there for business, but it's personal business. And not just that, it's actually *very* personal business—the kind of stuff you might avoid talking about elsewhere or, at least, not the kind of stuff you open conversations with.

Some clients will open by asking me how I'm doing. It's a lovely and polite thing to do, and yet, if I were to answer extensively, it would take away time and focus from the goals of the meeting.[100] So, if you start by asking your therapist how they are, it's nice, but it's a nonstarter.

I'm writing this chapter in response to a friend who asked, "Who should start talking? Or is there a less awkward way to start sessions?"

Let's start by addressing the awkwardness. *It's only awkward if you're confusing therapy with a normal adult human interaction.* Because it's not normal adult human interaction. It's somehow personal and professional at the same time. It often requires a deep human connection, yet the care flows only from them to you. It's time-limited. It's topic-limited. And it's all about you. It's exactly as weird as you think it is: You are sitting in a room trying to be vulnerable with a total stranger.

But that's the point: You are there to commune with yourself with the assistance of a second person. It's a time for your own introspection, for thinking and feeling through things, for analysis and resolution. The conversation exists only to serve your therapeutic goals.

---

100 To be clear, it's okay to ask your therapist how they're doing It's just not okay if their response makes it feel like you are now their therapist.

All that being said, I know most people feel awkward sitting in silence with someone else, especially at the beginning of a session. Now I'd like to review some of the ways a session gets started without endorsing any specific one. It's up to you to figure out what you prefer.

1. Show up with an agenda and launch into it.

How the session starts will be influenced by how you prepare for a session. (For more, see "How to Prepare for a Therapy Session" on page 183.) I've had clients who prepare an agenda and open the meeting by sharing it, choosing a topic, and jumping in. Treating therapy as a place of personal business is an efficient way to start. There's no awkward silence if you just get down to business right away.

2. Show up (intentionally) without an agenda and let your mind wander.

I have other clients who intentionally arrive without any plans, preferring to let themselves settle in, let their minds wander, or review previous topics with me, psychically wandering around until an agenda is discovered. While they have no plan in mind, in some sense, they do—the non-plan (sitting down and seeing what comes up) *is* the plan. You could announce this non-plan when you first sit down; then you might feel less awkward because now the silence in the room has context.

3. Show up (unintentionally) without an agenda and ask your therapist to start.

Why might someone do this? They could be feeling helpless ("Would you please start for me?"), aggressive ("Here—you start it!"), or simply open and wanting to collaborate ("How about you start, then let's see where I take it?").

The thing is, if you ask your therapist to start, now it's a question of how they respond. What are the therapist's options?

A) Say nothing at all. They might be doing so as a sign that it's your session and as a way of avoiding setting the agenda or tone. They want you to have the power. And yet, their silence can also feel like a power move,[101] which could increase the tension you feel in the room.

B) Say nothing, having previously let you know why that's what they will do. As a therapist committed to informed consent, I prefer it to Option A. In this way, my silence is meaningful rather than confusing and serves as a kind of prompt for the client.

C) Say, "It's quiet in here." I had a supervisor suggest this once, and my face got red just at the thought. Nothing (to me) is more awkward than commenting on the silence! So, why do it? It's a way of making an observation but not an interpretation. Again, it serves to prompt a response from the client.

D) Ask an opening question. I find that this is what most clients prefer. If you like this option, feel free to request it. Some therapists will be happy to oblige; hopefully, the ones who don't oblige will explain why (see Option B). There are a variety of opening questions, each of which sets the tone for the session. I'll provide some examples, again leaving it to you to reflect on your preferences:

    a) How are you today?
    b) How's your week been?
    c) Where do we begin?
    d) What would you like to do today?
    e) What would you like to work on today?

---

101 Jack Donaghy: "Whatever you do, don't speak first. Ninety percent of negotiations are lost by the person who speaks first. Because what is speaking a sign of?" (Long silent pause in the room.) Audience member: ". . . weakness?" Jack: "You—out. Fired." from Weiner, R. (Writer), & Richmond, J. (Director). (February 2, 2012). "Today You are a Man" (Season 6, Episode 5) [TV series episode]. In Fey, T. (Executive Productive), *30 Rock*. Broadway Video.

All of these are prompts for you to start talking. If you're not sure how to respond, you might feel awkward. I want to encourage you—it's okay not to have a response right away! A good therapist won't mind your silence and uncertainty; therapy is a place where mind-wandering and internal examination are appropriate and productive to a conversation.

In these first four options, the therapist is generally being nondirective and wanting you to be the one who leads. However, there is a fifth, more direct path your therapist could take:

E) Set the agenda themselves. This is a very strong opening, which has its drawbacks. By setting the agenda, they have freed you from figuring it out yourself . . . or deprived you of the opportunity to figure it out yourself. Please feel free to request this, but be aware that some therapists will comply and others will resist.

Finally, there's an option that is both directive and nondirective at the same time:

F) Offer a menu of openings. As a consent-oriented therapist, this is my most common opening. I'll say, "Well, we have a few options. We could sit here and just see what comes up; you could start talking about your week and see where that leads; or I can review the topics we discussed last week, and you'll see if you feel particularly drawn to one of them."

Now that you've read the above, you have two questions to consider:

1. How would you prefer to start?
2. If you want your therapist to start, how would you prefer they start?

The beauty of the weirdness in therapy is that "How do we start a session?" is actually a great topic of conversation in therapy. Ask them and see what they say. Discuss it together, figure out your preferences, find out theirs, then discuss what you might do next.

My main point: It doesn't have to be awkward! This is not a normal conversation, so if it feels unnatural, you're probably doing it right. In a normal conversation, it's awkward if you don't know what you're doing there; in therapy, being uncertain about what to do is extremely common. You're not supposed to be good at this.

It's awkward only if keeping up the flow of conversation is necessary for everyone's comfort. A good therapist understands and appreciates that a good therapeutic session isn't necessarily one that flows. We're aiming for comfortable silence here, one in which you feel free to go blank, to mind-wander, to take more time than is usually allowed in normal company.

So, if you know how you want to start, just go for it. If you're not sure how to start, I invite you not to treat this as a normal conversation and (sorry to my colleagues who feel differently) not treat your therapist as a normal person. You're not here for our entertainment or stimulation; we're here for you, and we're happy to wait, offer a prompt if requested, and comfortably muddle through the beginning right alongside you.

How to Remember to Do That Thing That Made Sense in Therapy

Insights Are Enough . . . Sometimes

I'm a cognitive[102] therapist (okay, cognitive behavioral[103]). This means that, besides the relational work essential to all good therapy, I mostly spend my day saying variations of "Yes, that makes sense, but what if you thought about this other way?" Ideally, the client arrives (whether on their own or assisted by me) at an insight that changes how they think about themselves, their world, their options, etc., which then changes how they act.

The insight itself can often be enough to make the change. I can tell if this will be the case when the client responds to an insight with "Oh. Ohhhhhh. Huh. Okay, yeah, hmmm, all right. Wow." The insight has sunk in and momentarily pushed aside their problematic thought patterns. The client might come back a week later saying something like "Every time I thought of doing [that bad habit], it just didn't make sense to be that way anymore" or "I keep hearing your words in my head." As a cognitive therapist, this is very gratifying to hear, and it sure does feel efficient. I shared a thought, and it made a difference—done and done!

---

102 My work with clients primarily focuses on identifying and changing thought patterns.
103 A therapeutic orientation that focuses on identifying and changing both thought-patterns and behavioral-patterns.

If only it were always so simple. Sometimes, the insight lands on the surface instead of sinking in. It took me a long time in the field to realize that hearing, "That makes sense," signaled *potential* progress rather than a triumphant therapeutic breakthrough. Making sense is not the same as making a difference. To put it another way, the insight reaches the client's head but not their heart. They come back the next week saying, "I didn't remember what we said. As soon as I left the session, I just went back to doing what I always do."

Why are insights often not enough? It shouldn't be that surprising. You have spent your whole life thinking and doing things in certain ways, and those ingrained views and habits are, predictably, *way* more powerful than some brilliant thing your therapist might say.

How do you go from making sense to making a difference? How do you turn a life-changing insight into actual life change? Basically, what can you do so you'll remember to do that thing that made sense in therapy?

Quick Caveat: Cognitive Behavioral Therapy (CBT) May Be the Wrong Medicine

I'm going to focus below on methods within CBT. But first, some important humility. If your state of mood or mind is particularly stuck in place, I recommend looking into therapies that don't rely so heavily on reasoning. Reasoning has a very limited impact when your body knows better—specifically if your body has a long history of depressive and anxious responses and/or when one or more traumatic experiences are involved.[104]

In those cases, I recommend looking into experiential therapies (IFS, EMDR, SP, AEDP, EFT, ECT, etc.—gonna leave it to you to google the acronyms) as well as psychiatric medication (when appropriate).

Now then . . .

104 Van der Kolk, B. A. (2014). *The Body Keeps the Score: Brain, Mind, and Body in the Healing of Trauma*. Viking.

Adopt and Adapt (and Attack!) the Insight

I have a saying inspired by my love of games: "It's worth twice as many points when the client says it." If your therapist offers an insight that you like, take immediate steps to make it your own. Talk about it, say what you like about it, explain what significance it has for you, and, above all, put it in your own words. When it comes out of your own mouth, you have **adopted** the insight as your own.

To personalize the insight further, you'll need to **adapt** it. You can adapt the insight by exploring how to apply it to the particular situations you're facing. To give an oversimplified example, the insight might be "Honesty is the best policy," and the adaptation is "Honesty is the best policy, except when . . ." Another common adaptation is to change the language offered by your therapist, who might be stuck in therapy-talk mode. Instead of asking your partner for a process conversation, you might reword the request to something like "Can we talk about how we're getting along?" or whatever language feels natural to you. (For more, see "Process Conversations: How to Practice Intersubjectivity Together" on page 162.)

These adaptations may arise out of your efforts to **attack** the insight. Sounding promising in therapy is different from working out in real life, so it's important for both you and the therapist to poke holes in the plan. While a good therapist will facilitate this part for you, they are still an outsider to your life, so they are less likely to know what will or will not work for you. So, ask yourself, "What's unrealistic here? What obstacles are we forgetting about?" You should be saying, "Hold on. This sounds great, but what about . . . " until you've run out of challenges. For example, "Hold on, honesty sounds great, but what about when it would get me in trouble? When it would hurt someone else? When there's no time?" And so on.

Once the insight has been adopted, adapted, and attacked, you are more prepared to apply it outside therapy sessions. You are ready for the next stage, which should be called "Planning to Practice." But it's more fun to call it . . .

How to Outrun the Zombies

I don't know why this is the example I always use. I guess I'm just tickled by it. Here it is: If you want to outrun the zombies, you have to start training before the zombie apocalypse starts. Do not assume you'll just be able to do it when the time has come.

In CBT, we refer to this kind of training as rehearsal: practicing skills in safe, controlled environments (a.k.a. limited exposure exercises) before the action plan is needed in prime time. Specifically, there are two major skills that require rehearsal (so you remember to do that thing that made sense in therapy): mindfulness and reframing.

- Mindfulness has many meanings, but here's how I'm using it: Mindfulness is the in-the-moment ability to recognize that you are in one of those situations in which you want to use the insight.
- Reframing is about training your mind to recognize problematic thoughts and to be ready with more productive, alternative ways to express that thought to yourself and others.

Without practicing in advance, it's unlikely you'll remember to be mindful or use reframing. Otherwise, when your various stress responses kick in, you go into autopilot, and all therapeutic insights go out the window.

Rehearsals: Limited Exposure Exercises

Whether you're looking to work on mindfulness or reframing (and often, it's both), you'll need an opportunity to try them out, ideally in a controlled environment in which struggle and failure don't matter. The whole point of rehearsal is that you're not good at this yet!

Here's one model for rehearsing both mindfulness and reframing: The exposure is either mentally conjuring up a stressful situation or exposing yourself to two to five minutes of relevant media that trigger stress responses. Here's what you'll do before, during, and after the exposure:

- Before: Practicing mindfulness of your default (pre-exposure) state.

  - Find a comfortable place to sit or lie down.
  - Slow your breathing and do whatever settling in means to you.
  - Once settled, scan your body to understand your current default state—the pace and quality of breath, muscle tension, or relaxation, whether it feels easy or difficult to remain still, etc.
  - Notice the quality of your thoughts as well. Does your mind feel busy, fast, slow, open, focused, free?

- During the exposure: Practicing mindfulness of in-the-moment changes.

  - Notice any changes to your bodily state—breathing, tension (shoulders, jaw, brow, hand)—and any agitation behaviors (tapping, balling fists, sighing, eye rolls, etc.).
  - Notice any changes to your mental state. Is your thought process accelerating? Are your thoughts more tinged with emotion? Notice any anxious/angry/disdainful thoughts that arise. Listen to yourself for knee-jerk verbal responses.

- After the exposure: Practicing relaxation, reflection, and reframing.

  - Relaxation: Assuming that the exposure caused some level of stress response, practice whatever relaxation techniques you discussed with your therapist. Practice them until you find your body more relaxed.[105]
  - Reflection: To remember to do that thing that made sense in therapy, you'll need to realize when it's time to do that thing. So, review your experiences during the exposure. What did you notice going on in your body and mind? What will be

---

105 If you find that the techniques aren't working, let your therapist know! Not every technique works for every person.

your internal signs that now is the time to use that thing you learned? What are the thoughts, feelings, and actions signaling that you're getting worked up?

- Reframing: Review the anxious/angry/disdainful thoughts that arose during the exposure. Write them down. Now, what was that reframe again? What was that thing the therapist said that sounded like a more helpful way of thinking here? Remember it, write it, say it aloud, and see if it changes how you feel.[106] Imagine yourself saying it in the actual situation and determine whether it comes out naturally.

In all of these exercises, the goal is to build awareness of *when* an insight is needed and to build that muscle for *how* you will apply the insight.

A Real-Life Rehearsal: Listening to Political Talk Radio

To show you how this works, I am providing an example from my personal therapeutic work. The issue at stake is my hot-headedness and my desire to learn to keep my cool when annoyed at others.

"That Thing that Made Sense in Therapy"

It's the insight that, when I'm arguing with people, I should remember to keep my calm rather than try futilely (and increasingly angrily) to get my point across. For the full insight, see "About to Talk with Someone Difficult? Bring These Two Goals" on page 146.

Planned Exposure

I will listen to five minutes of political talk radio, specifically a radio personality whose opinions I find wrong and obnoxious. I will keep the content vague in order to make my example relatable to any political orientation.

---

106 If you find that the reframe isn't working, let your therapist know! Not every reframe works for every person.

Before: Practicing Mindfulness of My Default State

I'm reclining on my couch. I can steady my breath. I feel myself relaxing into the couch, my muscles letting go, and a lovely sinking feeling of gravity pressing me lightly into the cushions. My face feels relaxed. Something inside me—I can't quite place it—is tingling though. I think this is because I know I'm about to subject myself to something stressful. My mind feels open, and I think it's because I'm getting myself motivated to do this exercise.

During: Practicing Mindfulness of In-the-Moment Changes

I start listening. The presenter is talking about the state of affairs and how various political figures are dealing with it . . . *What?* I find myself thinking, *How would that be your conclusion? That's mean-spirited. What an uncharitable and, frankly, cruel way of thinking of things.*

Okay, okay. I got caught up in the reaction. I need to pull back and just notice it. Well, thought-wise, my thoughts definitely sped up and escalated emotionally. I'm noticing not just my disgust but that I'm talking back, spouting judgments and counter-arguments. When I'm not speaking, my lips are pursed, my brow furrowed. The tingling in my body has become more pronounced—I feel it in my forearms, this kind of electric edginess. I remembered my breath just now—it's shallower than it was before.

After: Practicing Relaxation, Reflection, and Reframing

Relaxation: I turn the radio off and recline again—oh, huh. I hadn't noticed that I'd sat up when I got worked up listening to that . . . guy (the actual word that came to mind is a bit stronger). For me, relaxation is about flopping; I let my arms flop back beside me, palms up, and let my head loll to one side. I'm not holding myself up anymore. Having done so, I notice that my breath is returning to a deeper and more regular pace. I now realize that refocusing on my body interrupted the angry thoughts I was having.

Reflection: Well, what have I learned? Tension in my face and an electric edginess are the signals that I'm getting worked up. That and the upwelling of angry thoughts as I notice that I'm forming rebuttals and attacks.

Reframing: The angry/disdainful thoughts were: *This guy is an idiot, and I want to put him in his place. He should know better. It's not okay that other people listen and feel convinced by him. Now, what was that reframe again? Right—if I can't get through to him (and I don't expect I would, even if I called in to the station), it's really not worth my energy trying to. Instead, I can take some pride in handling myself better. He might be an idiot, but getting worked up like this is only hurting myself. What would I say if he were in front of me, if we were actually having this conversation, and I realized that it's no use arguing? I could say, "I don't expect to get anywhere with you on this, so I think I'm done discussing it." Or "I disagree, but I don't feel like trying to convince you—it's not worth my energy." Yeah—I think I could say the first one.*

Conclusion

If you want to remember to do that thing that made sense in therapy, make it your own by knowing how to explain it to yourself (adopt), how to change it as needed (adapt and attack), and practice, practice, practice (rehearsing mindfulness, relaxation, reflection, and reframing). Good luck!

One more note: If you want to plan to practice, you'll need a solid plan! It's not a real practice plan until you've thought through all the steps, written them down (digitally or on paper), put them on your schedule (for some, that's setting a specific time; for others, that's placing it between two activities already scheduled), and thought through how to address the internal and external obstacles that might arise.

It's Good to Question
Your Therapist

When Should You Question Your Therapist?

A friend recently posed this dilemma: As a client, sometimes their therapist makes a point that feels off the mark. What do they do in that situation? Push back? Go and find someone else? Be open to the expert seeing something they don't?

My friend is trying to solve the trick question at the heart of therapy: *Who is the expert in the room?* It's a false dilemma; both client and therapist must be treated as experts. The therapist better be some kind of expert in conducting therapy. After all, they went to school, got a degree, and expect to be paid. But the client must be treated as an expert as well because they will always know themselves longer and more intimately than the therapist ever can.

This is a conversation I conduct with every client during our first session. I ask, "Who's the expert in the room?" and then discuss what makes it a trick question. I say, "Who the hell[107] am I? No matter how well I get to know you, you will always know yourself better. I'm bringing this up now because whatever I say to you here, you're going to know whether I'm anywhere from 0 percent to 100 percent wrong, and you're going to know before I do. You can say, 'Yep, that's it,' or 'Nope, you're way off,' or 'Well, it's kinda like that. But really, it's more like this.' I need

---

107 That's not exactly the word I use.

you to feel comfortable telling me because whether I'm right or wrong, we're going to learn something that will serve our work. It's my job to handle your feedback well. You get to question, challenge, interrupt, redirect. *I* work for *you*. And this is how I treat my therapist, so don't worry, you get to do this to me."

In brief, what does this mean for my friend? It means that therapy should not be a power struggle. In my opinion as a therapist and as a client, a good therapist will respond to your questions graciously. So speak up! You'll find out what kind of therapist you have.

What's the Worst That Can Happen?

It will get ugly fast. Your therapist may move from an authoritative presence (holding expertise but focused on maintaining a good relationship) to an authoritarian one (focused on control). Distrust any therapist who gets defensive or aggressive in response to your questions. This indicates that they're reacting to your question as a power struggle. They will label you as "resistant" with the implication that, to make progress in therapy, all resistance is meant to be overcome.

They might try to use their position as an authority to silence you. Instead of allowing themselves to be vulnerable and open to questions or challenges, they are hiding behind their position. Distrust any therapist who tries to convince you by referencing their degrees, licenses, or the number of years they've practiced.

If this is how they respond, go find someone else.

What's the Best That Can Happen?

Your question should give your therapist pause. Or, better put, your therapist should instinctively pause after you ask your question. A good therapist experiences questions as important opportunities to strengthen the relationship and thereby make the work more productive. They should be thanking you for your question. They should try to understand your question before making their next move.

I once had a client get upset at me. When I asked why, it turned out to be a miscommunication. I had said that they were acting lovingly toward their family, and they took issue with the word *acting* as if I'd said they were *pretending* to be loving. Though that's not what I meant, it was a totally fair way to interpret what I'd said! I was really glad they spoke up. I agreed with their critique of my words, we brainstormed to find a less problematic phrase, and we moved on.

Sometimes, there's an actual difference in perspective. In this case, your therapist should be integrating your challenge into their point. You are bringing an angle (or at least a nuance) they didn't see, and they need to be open and humble enough to take your point. These are the words of a trustworthy therapist: "Hmm, okay. I think I see what you're saying. Let me try that again."

The Right Attitude for Therapy

Both client and therapist walk into the room expecting to both question and be questioned. A question can be an expression of curiosity or challenge. Either way, questions are helpful when they lead to greater collaboration in the room. I invite, encourage, and passionately request that my clients ask questions. Interrupt and challenge me, please!

The false dilemma (of who is the expert) is founded upon two conflicting virtues needed by both parties: boldness and humility.

Boldness is about speaking from your expertise. For the therapist, this includes expressing their point and having some trust in their instinctive and analytical responses to the client. For the client, this includes trusting and expressing your uncertainty and skepticism about your therapist's input.

Humility is about respecting the other's expertise. For both parties, this is not about being submissive but rather about remaining open and relational. Humble people remain curious and eager to have their awareness expanded beyond its current boundaries.

If everyone in the room can be both bold and humble while expecting the other to be bold and humble, you will get *so* much further.

If you can expect your therapist to respond humbly to questions, you will feel safe to question them. If you feel free to question, your therapist can enjoy the freedom of making bold statements.

A bold statement pays off, whether totally or partially right or wrong. If my instincts and analyses are correct, cool! I took a risk, and we made progress. If I'm anywhere from 1 percent to 100 percent wrong and you say so, hooray! Now we have an opportunity to talk it out. In doing so, we stumble our way toward greater insights.

So, definitely speak up and see what happens! Either way, you'll learn something important.

Start Process Conversations with Your Therapist

When we talk to each other, we're having a conversation. When we talk to each other *about how we talk to each other*, we're having a process conversation.

A process conversation is always initiated by a process comment—a statement that switches the focus of the conversation from the topic of conversation to how the conversation is going. If you and I are having a heated discussion and one of us says, "Wow, this discussion is getting really heated," that's a process comment! It's an opportunity to step aside from the heated discussion itself and try together to understand *why it's going the way it's going*. We're exploring the process by which our conversation has taken its shape, tone, direction, etc., with an eye toward improving it. Hopefully, by exploring how the conversation is going and how each of us contributes to it, we might figure out a more pleasant and productive way to communicate.

If it's not obvious yet, I'll say it—process conversations are (1) really valuable and (2) really hard to do well. A poorly held process conversation can be just as bad or worse than never having one at all. And that's why . . .

You should start process conversations with your therapist!

Why Have a Process Conversation with Your Therapist?

1. Because it's a relationship you're invested in. You want to get value out of your time and interactions. Therefore, it's important to get on the same page by asking questions: "What are we doing with my time in sessions? Are our interactions getting me further in my therapeutic goals?" Beyond asking questions, a process conversation is also a way of sharing critical feedback so your therapist knows what is and isn't working for you.
2. Because process conversations can be helpful everywhere in life, but therapy is hopefully the safest/easiest/most productive place to learn how to have them. Your therapist should be comfortable with and welcoming of process conversations. Meaning, they should have enough emotional and conversational intelligence to respond graciously and gracefully to process comments.
3. By developing your comfort level and skills for process conversations here, you've started preparing to initiate them elsewhere.

Maybe you're thinking, *Fine, I'll have a process conversation . . . But about what?*

About Therapy

Process conversations tend to be driven by curiosity and/or critical analysis. "Why is this going the way it's going?" Because criticizing can often (appropriately) seem confrontational, you might find it easier to start by asking process questions driven only by curiosity. Think of it as a check-in.

For example, in the first few sessions, you can ask:

*   "What do we do in sessions?"
*   "What's your [the therapist's] role?"
*   "How can I get the most out of these sessions?"

At periodic intervals (or as needed), you can continue this, asking:

- "How am I doing at this?"
- "How do you think it's going?"
- "How do I feel about our sessions?"
- "How do you feel about our sessions?"

Therapy is the process, and the conversation about the process hopefully helps you understand it better, giving you more power to get what you need from it.

About the Therapeutic Relationship

The therapeutic relationship is also a process of getting to know one another, identifying shared goals, then learning how to work together productively. Working together productively is not so simple! It's like carrying a couch up a stairwell[108]—a lot of communication will be required to accomplish it, and only tactful communication will accomplish it without leaving us hating each other at the end.

Process conversations about relationships are harder though, mostly because of the vulnerability required for all parties. Here are the beginnings of some process comments:

- "I liked it when you . . ."
- "It bothered me when you . . ."
- "I felt x when you . . ."
- "What did you mean by . . .?"

And those are only examples of process comments made in the aftermath of a conversation. Process comments can also be made in the

---

108 Varinaitis, A.S. (Writer), & Tsao, A. (Director). (1999, February 25). "The One with the Cop" (Season 5, Episode 16). In Bright, K.S., Kauffman, M, & Crane, D., (Executive Producers), *Friends*. Bright/Kauffman/Crane Productions.

middle of a conversation, which can be powerful but also increase the chance of feeling confrontational. For example:

- "Please don't interrupt me . . ."
- "That's not what I meant . . ."
- "Where are you going with this?"

Right? Did you get nervous just imagining saying (or being told) this? To tell someone how you feel about them and/or to have someone tell you how your actions affect them is intense, and it's a challenge to do it in a way that actually enriches the relationship. That's why you should try it in therapy, which is a safe space that makes it easier to be brave. Your first experience of a process conversation should feel rewarding! (For more, see "It's Good to Question Your Therapist" on page 209.)

Do(n't) Try This at Home!

At this point, I hope I've made the case for why process conversations are valuable and given you an idea of how to start one with your therapist.

Ideally, once you experience them for yourself, you'll want to have them with people in your life (outside therapy). But beware! A successful process conversation requires all parties to be ready, willing, and able to talk about the relationship itself for the purpose of improving it for all parties. Everyone needs to possess a bunch of emotional intelligence and communication skills and show up to the conversation intending to use that intelligence and those skills. Many people will not be able or want to do this, especially if they:

- Don't want to be vulnerable.
- Don't know how to respond when someone else is being vulnerable.
- Don't want to change the relationship.
- See any attempt to change the relationship as a power struggle.

This is why it's best to start in therapy. By getting real with the therapist, you'll practice opening this kind of conversation, have sensitive and assertive communication modeled for you by the therapist, and learn how to manage the emotional challenges throughout a process conversation.

In the healthy relationship section of this book, I develop this topic further, first by introducing intersubjectivity and then providing a step-by-step guide to having process conversations with people in your life.

"Is It Okay to Stop Growing?" When to End Therapy (At Least for Now)

Going In and Out of Therapy

Having entered therapy, clients often wonder whether, when, and how to exit. These are important questions! After all, if psychotherapy is a form of medicine, how long do you take it? If psychotherapy is a form of strength training, at what point do you (amicably) fire your personal trainer? This is when you say, "I've got it from here."

To be clear: For many people, going to therapy is a way of life rather than an on/off affair. They might be treating an ongoing condition, be on a lifelong journey of growth and healing, or just value the relationship and the ritual of therapy—a set time for personal reflection with the aid of a second person. It's okay to stay in therapy indefinitely!

For others, therapy is a temporary endeavor. They take it as needed. This kind of client may see a therapist for a while, feel done, then never come back. Or they may see one for a while, stop for a while, then start again when they feel it's needed.[109] Assuming they're getting what they're looking for each time, I believe the in-and-out-of-therapy style is a good fit for many potential clients.

---

109 A caution to the reader: Your most recent therapist may not have a schedule opening when you are ready to return.

Do You Feel Done?

How can you know when you're done with therapy, at least for now? Some questions to help you answer this question:

- How are you feeling in your everyday life?
- Are you finding that you have the personal tools you need (reflective skills, emotional management, action planning and taking) for the challenges that brought you to therapy?
- Are you running out of things to talk about in therapy?

If you're feeling good and aren't sure what to do next in therapy, congratulations! You might be done (for now and maybe forever).

But Is It Okay to Feel Done?

If you are asking yourself this question, maybe you feel hounded by an obligation toward your unlimited potential that's pushing you to always improve yourself. Beware of this trap! If someone tells me I have unlimited potential, I don't feel inspired—I feel exhausted. Unlimited self-improvement is neither possible (because of limited time, interests, and capabilities) nor desirable ("Wait, do I have to spend *every* waking moment making the most of myself?"). It might sound unfortunate to waste potential, but it's a special kind of perfectionistic torture to try to actualize every last drop of your potential.

In my professional opinion, it all comes down to distress and dysfunction. If you're not distressed (and not losing functions), you don't have to keep going. I've had clients who have come and gone, working on one piece at a time, and come back only when they feel some internal pressure to push forward. It can be a powerful expression of self-acceptance to allow yourself to feel done.

Does Your Therapist Think You're Done?

And what if your therapist thinks you're *not* done? You might think, *They are the authority, right? Maybe they know better than I do.* And they might. But, to be honest, many of us therapists have a built-in bias toward growth and healing. It kinda comes with the profession.

Even if your therapist thinks you should continue, they should express that sentiment without pressuring you. They should still be consent-oriented. (For more, see "10 Ways to Tell If Your Therapist Honors Consent" on page 177.) Ideally, they will provide you with a menu of options for moving forward, including pausing or stopping therapy altogether. Your therapist can offer pathways to further growth and healing, explaining what they are and why they might be useful. But you don't owe your therapist anything.

A Lifelong Journey, In or Out of Therapy

Even if your therapist is not encouraging you to stay, it can be hard for a client to leave. The therapist and therapy often represent values of growing, healing, or even just maintaining mental wellness.

But! You can and should express those values (healing, growth, and maintenance) for the rest of your life as well. You can pursue your growth, healing, and general mental wellness in a variety of ways. As a CBT-oriented therapist, isn't that what I'm trying to convey to all my clients? I want you to become your own resource—well-equipped with tools for reflection, emotion, and action.

Ultimately, you do the work in the way and time that works for you. A therapist can be a key part of that work at times, but they don't have to be. Therapy is only one method of doing intentional work toward growth and healing.

CONCLUSION

Living Well Among the Trees, Gazing over the Forest

Among the Trees

In a sprawling forest, you can wander for days and never see the same sight twice. That's not the case here. While you do roam all over, you also crisscross the same areas over and over, and it takes a while before you start recognizing them. Once you start recognizing parts of the forest, you can begin tracing and retracing your steps, starting to understand how one thing leads to another and how paths join, split, overlap, run parallel, etc. Once you have a sense of the paths, you can start planning routes. You can wander, explore, chart, and have adventures (good and bad ones).

And you're not the only one in there! Depending on where you're walking and looking, you might notice fellow travelers. They may be a welcome or unwelcome sight, depending on what kind of journeyer you are and what kind of journey you are on. But, if you both are so inclined, you can stop and compare notes. Do your maps align? What details are you each missing? What details do you think the other got right or wrong? Are you going in similar directions, and would it make more sense to start traveling together?

The more you travel the forest and reflect on your wanderings, the better you are at finding what you're looking for and making yourself at home.

Wise and Courageous Living

In this book, I have shared some of my notes on what I've found so far as a fellow traveler and as a therapist to fellow travelers.

I have demonstrated the value in getting up close to the trees through attention to detail, nuance, and the interplay between things. Knowing distinctions among words enables you to better label and categorize your experiences. By embracing your inner turmoil, you start to see how your emotions contain their own wisdom but also require wisdom to be handled gracefully. Slowing down, looking closely, and looking again, you notice the little ways you cooperate and struggle with others, and you can see the actions and reactions that enhance or harm your relationships.

I have also demonstrated the value of trying to take in the forest as a whole, or at least large regions of it—to experience life as an immense reality awash in philosophical themes like meaning, responsibility, time, goodness, connection, and disconnection. A greater orientation emerges, enabling you to recognize where you're wandering (and what you're stepping in).

With themes colored in and details marked—a.k.a. combining the understanding of both the forest and the trees—you can make quite the map of life, its situations, its concerns, etc. Your map ranges widely and contains many insets.

But that's all conceptual, and what matters most is what happens existentially—what happens to your sense of life and how you want to live it. Through reflection and analysis, by learning to zoom in and zoom out, you learn to show up to life with curiosity, with careful and caring attention (in relation to the trees) and with awe and humility (in relation to the forest). It takes more than orientation to make your way through life; it takes courage to actually navigate, try things out, let yourself make mistakes, allow for failure, and try again. Looking at life is not enough; you're here to live it. With greater clarity for your inner and outer worlds, you can prepare emotionally to take on challenges and find satisfaction in achieving your goals.

I'll acknowledge that I've covered only patches of the forest in this book. I'm missing key details and patterns. Some parts of the map are still labeled "Here be dragons," words that alternatingly repel and attract my attention. There's a lot more to be explored, experienced, and mapped. And thank goodness! For me, exploration is most of the fun.

I'm not done exploring. I'll keep at it, and I'll let you know what I find. Oh hey!—if you're a fellow traveler, why don't you do some exploring and let *me* know what *you* find?

Over the Forest

I invite you to take one last look. Imagine you are flying a drone over it all, surveying from above so it feels like you are hovering and gazing upon life.

It's so big! It's just as overwhelming to try to take it all in as it is to be in it. It's a sublime feeling—somehow both beautiful and terrifying.

Deep breath.

The forest itself has a life of its own. From here, you can see lush areas, dry patches, signs of past disturbances, and areas of new life. Oh! Look there—you can see that the seasons are changing. Do you remember what it looked like last season? Can you imagine what it will look like next season? Will you still recognize the same places as they change from desolate to vibrant to lush to decomposing? What storms lie ahead, and what new perks and pitfalls will emerge in their wake? What opportunities exist?

Whatever the season, the plan is the same: to feel lost and confused, explore and gain clarity, and gain satisfaction in that new clarity until the next thing comes and confuses you again. To feel comfortable in both orientation and disorientation.

It's certainly an adventure!

Acknowledgments

Thanks to my mother and father, who have encouraged me to an irresponsible degree (and supported me through several more degrees) and kept me grounded in reality.

Thanks to Naomi, whose bravery inspires me every day and who reminds me to do things besides think, write, and talk.

Thanks to my creative director, Howard Van Es of Let's Write Books, Inc., who gets me and, fortunately, also gets what a professionally crafted book looks and sounds like. (Also thanks to Miriam Zaslow and Sara Khodorovsky for the assist!)

Thanks to my awesome beta readers—Stacy Horn, R.L. Kramer, Jesse Martin, Yonah Meiselman, Joshua Rosenthal, Sammy Sass, Renee Vanderstelt, and Carl Vitullo. Thanks for catching that. I totally missed it!

Thanks to my peer supervision group—Kaleigh Bergeron, Emmeline Kim, Andrea Randall, and Ruby Yarmush. You are the four I wanted to keep working with after grad school ended, and dammit, I meant it.

Thanks to Tasha Chemel, Etye Greentree, Rabbi Suzie Jacobson, Dr. Natalie Russ, Rabbi Ari Saks, and Yotam Schacter for the conversations I live for, many of which influenced this work.

Thanks to Zoe Jack and Dr. Heidi Schreiber-Pan for both employing me and goading me ever onward.

Thanks to all my clients—the inspiration and ultimate audience for everything here.

Thanks to Amazon.com, whose techno-feudalism may be a problem for society but made this book way easier to produce than actually getting the attention of a publishing company.

Thanks to that which creates, connects, and destroys us all.

Resource Guide

For more on honoring the contradictions and tensions of life, check out:

Barrett, W. (1990). *Irrational Man: A Study in Existential Philosophy.* Anchor Books.

Erasmus, D. (1958). *The Praise of Folly.* [Ann Arbor], University of Michigan Press.

Kegan, R. (1994). *In Over Our Heads: The Mental Demands of Modern Life.* Harvard University Press.

Schwartz, R. C. (2021). *No Bad Parts: Healing Trauma and Restoring Wholeness with the Internal Family Systems Model.* Sounds True.

Watts. A. (2011). *The Wisdom of Insecurity: A Message for an Age of Anxiety.* Vintage Books.

For more on the power of existential thinking for self-understanding, check out:

Barrett, W. (1990). *Irrational Man: A Study in Existential Philosophy.* Anchor Books.

May, R. (1969). *Love and Will.* W. W. Norton.

For more on the power of metaphor for self-understanding, check out:

Gillman, N. (1990). *Sacred Fragments: Recovering Theology for the Modern Jew.* Jewish Publication Society.

Lakoff, G., & Johnson, M. (1981). *Metaphors We Live By.* University of Chicago Press.

For more on improving interpersonal communication, check out:

Benson, B. (2019). *Why We Yell: The Art of Disagreement*. Public Affairs.
Rosenberg, M. B. (2003). *Nonviolent Communication: A Language of Life* (2nd ed.). PuddleDancer Press.

For some fun reads that inspire my thinking in general, check out:

Escher, M.C., & Locher, J.L. (1974). *The World of M.C. Escher*. H. N. Abrams.
Irwin, W., Conard, M.T., & Skoble, A.J. (2001). *The Simpsons and Philosophy: The D'oh! of Homer*. Open Court.

About the Author

Matthew Lowe is a licensed psychotherapist with a master's degree in mental health counseling from William James College. He has practiced psychotherapy for over ten years at multiple substance abuse treatment centers, colleges, and private practice venues.

Before his current work, Matthew was a public school health educator and religious school philosophy teacher. He received a master's degree in theological studies at Harvard Divinity School and bachelor's degrees in philosophy at Columbia University and the Jewish Theological Seminary.

Matthew lives outside Baltimore with his partner Naomi and dog Prinsesstårta.

Find out more about Matthew at
www.facebook.com/MatthewLoweAuthor
and www.instagram.com/MatthewLoweAuthor

www.ingramcontent.com/pod-product-compliance
Lightning Source LLC
Chambersburg PA
CBHW060019100426
42740CB00010B/1526